PUT TO THE TEST

'The book is a must for anyone who wants to relive an important part of post-war cricketing history.'
Colchester Evening Gazette

'Altogether ... makes quite revealing and compelling reading.'
The Citizen, Gloucester

'Yorkshire cricket lovers will find Geoff Boycott's first book very revealing ... His account of the tour is an admirably detailed report of a series of cricket matches. The fireside cricket lover can relive a fascinating series of tight encounters.'
Sheffield Morning Telegraph

'Coming from England's senior professional and outstanding batsman, the observations and comments are particularly interesting.'
Yorkshire Gazette & Herald

Put to the Test

by GEOFF BOYCOTT

SPHERE BOOKS LIMITED
30/32 Gray's Inn Road, London WC1X 8JL

First published in Great Britain by
Arthur Barker Ltd, 1979
Copyright © Geoff Boycott and Terry Brindle 1979
Published by Sphere Books Ltd, 1980

TRADE
MARK

Set in Linotype Granjon

Typeset in Great Britain by Northumberland Press Ltd,
Gateshead, Tyne and Wear
Printed in Canada

Contents

Introduction

It was indicative of the high standard which Geoffrey Boycott has established over the years that many critics were prepared to write him off after last winter's Australian tour.

By his own severely self-critical standards – and by the standards others have come to expect – Boycott's figures in Australia were unflattering. But those who expected one disappointing tour to dull his appetite for the game were disillusioned last summer.

Boycott's reaction was typically Boycott. For the second time in his career, he finished with a first-class average of over 100 runs; he was again the leading English batsman in the national averages and led Yorkshire's batting averages by well over 50 runs.

Not a bad season for a man who was supposed to have left his best years back in Adelaide or Melbourne ... and if Boycott the bowler had taken one more wicket for the first-class averages, he would have topped those, too !

The tour which England undertook last winter may be the last involving Test cricket as it has been recognised over the years. Established cricket's peace with Kerry Packer – albeit an uneasy and even unsatisfactory peace – opens the door to the hard sell and razamatazz which characterised World Series Cricket.

Matches under lights ... coloured clothing ... a heavy accent on advertising – all are likely to become established in Test cricket before long. It is an intrusion which many, including Boycott himself, will view with some regret.

Boycott is amongst the most conservative of cricketers: the first to speak out publicly when Establishment cricket needed a spokesman, the last of the world's leading batsmen to adopt a crash helmet. There is something faintly ridiculous in the thought of Boycott clad in dark blue accessories for the benefit of the television cameras.

But cricket will evolve, even if it does not always seem to progress. Boycott's view of the 1978–9 tour may, in retrospect, be a last look at a traditional form of Ashes cricket doomed to be overtaken by the tide of commercialism.

TERRY BRINDLE

1 Bon Voyage ...

It was hardly the best preparation for a four-month tour of Australia.

England had taken the vice-captaincy from me, my Mother had died and then Yorkshire announced they no longer wanted me as captain ... any one of those problems would have been quite enough to contend with on the eve of the most difficult tour in cricket, and I was saddled with all three in the space of six weeks.

You can imagine my state of mind when we finally flew out of Heathrow. On second thoughts, you can't – I doubt if anyone could really appreciate just how dispirited and confused I felt at that moment. My mind was in a whirl, decisions had to be made which would affect my whole future and still I was conscious of the need to clear my head and concentrate on the job in hand. Even now I find it difficult to sort out the threads.

The vice-captaincy business was a puzzling about-turn. In May I was captain of England, having taken over when Mike Brearley was injured in Pakistan and led the side through New Zealand; there was even some speculation about whether Mike would get the job back. I expected that he would because it would have been very unfortunate to lose the best job in the world through injury and, of course, once he was fit again Mike was reinstated.

But when Mike hurt his arm and had to miss the first one-day Test against Pakistan, the selectors were most anxious that I should play and I captained the side. I wasn't completely fit myself, having ricked my back bowling for Yorkshire, but they were keen that I should play.

From the end of May to the middle of September – and we are talking about months not years – the situation had done a complete circle. From being vice-captain and England captain when they needed one, I had been relegated to the ranks. It was an about-turn which I certainly didn't expect.

That was why I asked to see Alec Bedser, the chairman of selectors, and the tour manager Doug Insole. I needed to get my position clear and I wanted a few answers. We talked it over and they put their point of view – partly, as Alec had already told the Press, that they wanted me to concentrate on my batting. It struck me that I had been accused of concentrating too much on my batting in the past but no matter, the conversation was valuable and I still wanted to go to Australia.

Alec also said publicly that they wanted me to score a century in every Test match. I'm sure he meant it as a compliment but it was a pretty tall order to say the least – I seem to remember a guy called Bradman who could bat a bit and he never managed that kind of sequence on tour. Still, I meant to have a darned good try and my record over the past two seasons with Yorkshire and England worked out at one century in every four innings. A bit Bradmanesque; perhaps a good omen.

No sooner had I come to terms with the England situation than I was confronted with the worst day of my life. My Mother died.

She had been ill for some time, years in fact, so to that extent I suppose her death was not unexpected. But somehow you never really come to terms with the fact that it will happen, however much you try to adjust your mind to it.

Mum had cancer, she fought against it with amazing courage but it was terminal and we all knew it. All through the 1978 season her condition deteriorated from day to day; the doctors didn't know how long she had to live but they could not hold out any hope. It was just a matter of time.

That was one of the reasons why I had to have a meeting with Alec Bedser and Doug Insole before the tour got under way. In the first place there was a real possibility that I would have to stay at home. With my Mother fading so fast I really didn't relish the prospect of clearing off to Australia and leaving her not knowing whether she would live a week or a month.

And if I decided to go on tour it would have to be understood that I might have to come home if her condition became critical. I didn't know how England would react to that. They might want me to fly out and join the tour later or they might simply rule me out altogether and take someone else. I had accepted a place on the tour so I obviously had responsibilities to England but I also had to decide in my mind where I wanted to be. It was terribly confusing, and difficult.

I know other people face this kind of situation in life and come to terms with it, but my position was a bit different from most. My Father died eleven years ago so I was virtually the head of the family – and the only member of the family still living at home. We were very close, my Mother and I, and I relied on her a lot.

It is always a hard thing to lose a very special parent. If you are married and live away from home it is bad enough, but it is a dreadful experience to live with someone you love and see them deteriorate from week to week. She insisted on being at home though she had been in hospital for treatment many times, and naturally we respected her wishes. The family rallied round and we never left her in the house alone, which naturally involved everyone in a great deal of to-ing and fro-ing. It was a demanding, emotionally fraught situation to say the least, and when I had time to think about the tour situation I couldn't see any simple solution. There was no way of knowing what her condition would be from day to day.

On Wednesday September 27th my Mother died at home in Fitzwilliam and two days later I went to Yorkshire's end-of-season meeting at Headingley.

It has been suggested that Yorkshire offered me a postponement in view of my Mother's death, but I want to put the record straight on that one. The day after my Mother died the Yorkshire secretary Joe Lister rang my home and spoke to one of my brothers. Joe said he wanted to speak to me but as I wasn't in at the time he was told I would be back about 4.30 pm.

I rang Joe at 4.30: he wasn't in, but finally contact was established at about 5.30 pm. Joe was very kind and sympathetic and he asked me whether or not I was going to the Yorkshire meeting which was due to take place the following day. Once I said that I would be at the meeting there was no suggestion that it might be put back.

Yorkshire appoint their captain for one season only, so each year for the past few years I had attended the meeting of the cricket committee and left the room while the captaincy was being discussed. That has become the routine since the captain was co-opted on to the committee.

I went to Headingley with my mind in a daze. My Mother's death was still very much in my mind, of course, and there were a thousand things to do at home; the tour was only three weeks away. I hoped to heaven it was going to be a routine meeting.

We had the usual cricket committee meeting and then the cricket chairman John Temple asked me to leave while they discussed the captaincy. Nobody had mentioned the captaincy up to then or asked me any questions about it.

I never went back into the room and the cricket committee went straight in to lunch at the end of their meeting. Temple told me their decision would have to go before the general committee that afternoon for ratification; he didn't tell me what the decision was but I knew something was wrong, if only because in previous years he had often given me a hint that the cricket committee's recommendation was for my reappointment.

It felt very strange. Nobody from the cricket committee spoke to me; in fact the only people who exchanged a few words were general committee members arriving for lunch prior to their meeting in the afternoon. I finished up sitting on my own in the dining room.

The general committee met and I waited outside. John Temple offered to ring me at home with the decision, which I thought was a bit strange because it had never been suggested in the past, but I said I preferred to stay. If they wanted me they knew where I was. The captaincy was down as the last item on the agenda but they agreed to take it first so that I wouldn't have to hang about for four hours.

I waited in the members' bar, wondering what was going on, trying to remember what I had to do next at home. The house would have to be cleared because it was common knowledge that I was going to be away for four months and there was a lot of valuable stuff to go into store as well as numerous items of sentimental value. And then there were the funeral arrangements ...

John Temple came out, told me that I had been replaced as captain and said he was going to telephone John Hampshire with the news. I don't remember his exact words.

It didn't seem unreasonable to want to know why I had been replaced, but no one seemed inclined to offer any explanation. Considering that nobody had tried to discuss my captaincy during the season, at the end of the season or during the committee meeting that morning, I felt I was entitled to hear some sort of reason for their decision.

John Temple agreed when I asked him if I could meet a deputation of the committee, but I had to wait until the general committee had finished their business. So I ended up sitting at Headingley all afternoon after all.

Then I had a meeting with Temple, the club chairman Arthur Connell and the president Sir Kenneth Parkinson. They gave their views, I gave mine, but obviously the decision had been taken and there seemed to be nothing we could say there to change it. In any case I was in no frame of mind to have a proper discussion about anything; I just asked a few questions and listened to the answers. My mind was too full to take it all in.

The decision was announced to the Press that night and over the weekend a Reform Group, which had been created some time earlier, proposed to call for a special meeting and challenge the committee. I will always be grateful for the loyalty and support which so many people showed but at that time I was in no state to think about Reform Groups or anything else.

I had been demoted by England and had now lost the Yorkshire captaincy three days before we buried my Mother. What was it one newspaper said? 'It was the sort of thing you would not do to a stray mongrel dog in the back streets of Leeds ...' I felt that just about summed it up.

For a week I was inundated with telephone calls and besieged by the media. Everyone wanted a story (which is natural enough) but there was not a lot I could say or wanted to say; I'm not sure I would have been too rational at the time. The only newspaper I spoke to was the *Yorkshire Post* until a week later I appeared on Mike Parkinson's TV show. And that caused a bit of a row.

Many people have criticised me for appearing on the show; they reckon I didn't do myself or my cause any good. But I was wary. I knew I would have to say something and I certainly didn't want to go through the chore of talking to twenty or thirty journalists, repeating the same story time after time while they all tried to dig for something new, something different. And quite frankly I was afraid of being misquoted; there are some journalists whose motives I do not trust.

My decision to go on TV had nothing to do with money. I turned down an offer of over £10,000 to write an article for a national newspaper and for appearing on Parky's show I received the standard fee which is £100. Parky never mentioned money and I never discussed it with him; it simply wasn't important.

What I thought was important was to get my views over to millions of people who seemed to be interested and TV appeared to be the right medium for that. But naturally, you can't say everything you would like or explore every aspect of a question in twenty minutes or so, and with a topic as important as Yorkshire cricket we could have done with three hours, more, half a day.

The programme was intended to show how I felt about the situation and there was no way we could explore every ramification in twenty minutes. I tried to answer the questions as they came up, though every answer immediately prompted five more questions because the issue is such a deep one. I tried to crystallise my feelings and if I didn't succeed completely I don't think I failed completely either.

People wanted to know if I was going to Australia so I told them; they wanted to know what was going through my mind and I tried to tell them that, too. I was asked about the Yorkshire committee and I made myself clear then as I have since.

The Yorkshire committee is a very powerful body, making decisions which have far-reaching effects not only on the 11,250 members of the club but on thousands of others who support Yorkshire at the turnstiles or take a very personal interest in the affairs of the club. Many of the Yorkshire committee are sincere people who genuinely put the best interests of the club before their own ambition or sense of social status.

But not all are that trustworthy – and the untrustworthy members seem to hide behind the mere fact that they are committee. They justify every decision simply by saying it is a committee decision but they must know that being a member of any committee does not give them the magic power to be infallibly right. So when Yorkshire reflected critically on my record as captain by sacking me from the job I felt I was entitled to challenge their record of loyalty to the team.

Where was I going to say my piece? When and how? I might have gone on two or three TV programmes but I chose Parky's show because he is a friend and a man I can trust. People have said I chose Parky because he is a fan. OK – why shouldn't I prefer to put my point of view over in an atmosphere which was sympathetic rather than hostile?

But Parky is also a journalist and he had no intention of spoiling his reputation by asking questions which did not reflect what people were thinking and wondering. If anyone suggests that Parky gave me an easy ride because of our friendship they are talking rubbish.

Some of his questions were pretty pointed and perhaps I should not have given the forthright answers I did. But I am a cricketer, not a politician – and rather proud of the fact. And if the whole thing was some sort of set-up between friends, how did I manage to cause such a stir with my answers?

One point which needs clearing up is the remark I made about Mike Brearley, a throwaway remark which was reported in some newspapers as though I said it with calculated malice.

The Parkinson show is recorded – in fact the Press were allowed to watch the recording being made so they could get their stories in the Sunday papers – and before it starts the audience is 'warmed up' to encourage the right atmosphere and help everybody relax. We had the warm-up but just as the show was about to start there was a technical hitch which took the edge off the atmosphere; everybody felt a bit of an anti-climax. Parky began to chat to the audience and somebody called out 'Good luck in Aussie, Geoff. Get a lot of runs', or something like that. I shouted back 'I'll get more than Mike'

Brearley', and everyone accepted it as a friendly off-the-cuff remark intended to be amusing. It was no more than that and it certainly was not intended to be any sort of dig at Mike. I don't think anybody in the audience thought it was.

But Ted Dexter did – or at least he tried to make it sound as though I had had a real go at Brearley in an article he wrote next day. That article was a disgrace. If that's what a public school and university education does for Ted Dexter, I'm glad I went to Hemsworth Grammar School.

Yorkshire reacted to the Parkinson show by asking for a meeting as a matter of urgency and after an exchange of letters the meeting was fixed for the day before I left for Australia. It was the worst possible day for me and not, I may add, of my choosing.

My solicitor, Duncan Mutch, came with me to the meeting at 4 o'clock and addressed the committee for almost two hours, in almost complete silence from beginning to end. We had prepared a dossier which included letters and records showing how some committee men had been devious and disloyal over the years when I was captain of the side. I could have furnished them with a lot more evidence but, on reflection, I doubt if they intended changing their minds whatever was said. Once Duncan had said his piece they asked us to leave and we sat in an office adjoining the kitchens at Headingley while they chewed it over.

Then we went back in and Arthur Connell made a statement which was more or less the same one – with a few deletions and amendments – which was later given to the Press.

Connell told the Press:

The committee have discussed at length the representation which Mr Boycott's solicitor made on his behalf and re-affirm their decision. In the first place I would like to deal with the constitutional position.

This committee is elected by the members and everyone in this room has been so elected within the last three years, with the exception of the nominee of the Leeds Cricket, Football and Athletic Company. The committee's task is to run the club on behalf of the members and it is primarily responsible to the members for the decisions which it makes. I may say that it is the intention of the committee to take as early an opportunity as possible to put the matter before the members.

It does not have to justify its decisions to its employees but if a decision affects an employee personally he is entitled to know the reason why the decision was taken.

Let me say in the first place that this is nothing to do with playing ability; playing ability is irrelevant except insofar as a player must be good enough to be a member of the team before he can be considered. It is nothing to do with what Mr Boycott has done or has not done. It is to do with what he is.

Captaincy requires playing skill, technical ability and experience but is above all a matter of leadership and the ability to persuade the other members of the team to play right up to, and on occasions beyond, their potential. This is the quality which in the honest and sincere opinion of a majority of this committee Mr Boycott lacks.

He is so dedicated to the perfection and exploitation of his own batting technique that he is sometimes oblivious to the feelings and aspirations of his team mates and as a result he cannot and does not get out of his team what is there to be got.

You may think that the committee have taken a long time to reach this decision and indeed we have been criticised for this. His lack of leadership ability has been the question mark which has hung over his captaincy from early days.

It has come up every year – and I would emphasise that the appointment of a captain is made for one season only with no guarantee of continuance – and has been one of the principal factors which has been considered each year when the committee came to decide whether the incumbent captain was the best available, what were the alternatives and whether the time was right for a change to be made. The feeling has varied from year to year but this year a substantial majority decided that a change should be made. It was not a personal decision; it was made honestly and sincerely in the best interests of Yorkshire cricket.

However, this characteristic of utter dedication, which frequently leads to an inability to achieve personal relationships and so disqualifies the possessor from leadership, is nevertheless the quality which has enabled Mr Boycott to make himself the player which he is.

It is because he is so good a player and because of his constant and, I am sure, sincere assertion that all he wants is the best for Yorkshire cricket that the committee has offered him – and I have confirmed the offer – the maximum contract given to any of the playing staff, that is to say two years.

The committee hope that Mr Boycott will continue to play for Yorkshire – the general committee are unanimous on that point – and still hope that he may come to see that this is how he can best serve the county.

Finally, the committee wish to state that the new captain John Hampshire will have their unanimous support.

An interesting point about that statement is that it appeared to have been prepared before the meeting actually took place. Yorkshire presumably felt they ought to have something ready for the Press, but the way the statement was couched makes it pretty clear they had no intention of seeing our point of view, no matter what we said.

The Press naturally wanted some sort of statement from me, the TV people wanted me in front of the cameras. It was all hell let loose and my head was throbbing by the time I finally got out of Headingley after 10 o'clock and drove home.

I had to pack, there were a thousand and one domestic details to be seen to, it was after midnight but I still couldn't get to bed. The weeks since the end of the season seemed to be one long catalogue of chaos and turmoil – not exactly the best way to prepare for an Australian tour and the worst possible situation for me. I like to find solitude before a big tour, to think purely about my cricket and get myself in just the right frame of mind to play well. Everything seemed hopelessly, worryingly wrong when I finally got to bed and snatched five hours' sleep – and when I got up next morning there was a photographer perched outside my house waiting for a 'new' picture.

I started the tour well. I missed the train to London and no bloody wonder!

2 Hello Rodney Hogg!

Adelaide is a city of beautiful parks, good people and bad memories.

Clive Radley isn't likely to forget Adelaide quickly, or remember it with any great affection after his experience in the first State match of the tour. England could hardly feel pleased with themselves after losing to South Australia by 32 runs. And my memories of Adelaide will always, I suppose, be coloured by a certain incident in 1971 after a particularly galling run-out decision . . . But that is history.

We arrived in Adelaide in good spirits despite the jet-lag and the unavoidable hassle of twenty-nine hours' travelling. I enjoy travelling but twenty-nine hours is quite enough of a good thing. We were treated to a particularly distinguished film on the jumbo . . . something about a kangaroo called Matilda who finished up boxing for the world heavyweight championship. Might have been a true story; at least we got a few hours' sleep.

Adelaide is the perfect spot to start an Australian tour. It is a beautiful city, green and spacious, wrapped around parks and fountains. And the Adelaide Oval is a fine ground – ivy-covered walls on the outside, a bit like Wimbledon, and a picturesque playing area open on two sides. The sort of ground where it is easy to forget you are only a quarter of a mile from a bustling city centre.

The temperature at Adelaide is pleasantly warm in October even though the nights are cool and the breeze can be deceptively sharp. And the nets are invariably good. Had we started at Melbourne we would have been lucky to get any practice in at all because of their wet weather, Brisbane would have been far too hot and the wickets at Perth would have been too quick to help early acclimatisation.

So Adelaide was ideal, a relatively gentle introduction to

Australia in a city which is far more easy-paced than most State capitals. Certainly not as big and hectic as Sydney or Melbourne. Just the sort of place to overcome the effects of jet-lag and start concentrating the mind on four months' cricket.

Inevitably we all had problems adjusting to Australian time. I kept waking up in the early hours of the morning after about six hours' sleep, which was hopeless, and Bob Willis got so fed up with lying awake that he used to get up in the early hours and go for a run in the park opposite our hotel. He was like the headless horseman pounding past everybody's window.

There was a tremendous feeling of responsibility in the side, a sense that this tour was especially important. Packer was playing his World Series Cricket matches while we were in Australia and it was inevitable that there would be comparison between us and them, not just in the media but by the public at large. The Press described ours as the most important tour England had ever undertaken; we didn't really see ourselves as missionaries for established cricket but I suppose that's what we were. Nobody underestimated the significance of the next four months.

Doug Insole emphasised the importance of the tour when we met for the off at Lord's but he also suggested that we should compete with WSC by playing tough, positive traditional cricket rather than by trying to match Packer for 'fours and sixes'. That's the kind of superficial statistical game they enjoy playing but it's not really what winning the Ashes is all about.

Doug also touched on the difficult question of our relations with the WSC players. Many of them would be county team-mates of the England players – none from Yorkshire I'm glad to say – and they would naturally want to meet and mix. But Doug reminded everyone that the Press would be watching the situation very closely, and urged that we shouldn't do anything which might embarrass ourselves or the team. It seemed like sensible advice to me.

The vice-captain Bob Willis added a word of warning about the Aussie Press. We have some pretty sharp operators ourselves but the Aussies are past masters at seizing on one fact, or half a fact, and making it into a sensational story. They don't do it maliciously but by heaven they do it well. Or badly ...

And Mike Brearley emphasised the need for communication within the team. He felt that on a long tour players sometimes became disgruntled because they felt they were being left out of things; it was easy to form cliques without being aware of it and that wouldn't do team spirit any good. There would be pressure enough without creating any of our own.

We soon found out how true that was. The match against South Australia should have been the perfect pipe-opener to the tour: a decent pitch and opposition provided by what is regarded as the weakest of the mainland State sides. They had lost several of their best players – the Chappells, Cosier, Hookes – and while we were in Adelaide they were beaten pretty convincingly by Queensland in a Gillette Cup tie. Just the boost our confidence needed – and we lost the match by 32 runs.

Over-complacency? Perhaps there was a touch of that but not much. The fact is that it is always difficult to play well in the first match of the tour, no matter how much practice and how many nets you have to build up to it. Players are rusty after a six-week break following the English season; bowlers struggle to get loose and batsmen need to resharpen their timing.

That's why I didn't put too much importance in all the talk about how England were hot favourites for the Ashes. Even the Aussie Press were backing England to win the series and that's a distinctly ominous sign. I knew from experience that every match would be hard – and I never underestimate the Aussies' ability to produce a surprise fast bowler or two.

I remember meeting this quick bowler in Perth in 1970–1. Nobody had heard of him but his first delivery took my cap with it, bounced twice and smashed into the sightscreen eighty yards away. Hello Dennis Lillee.

So I wasn't altogether surprised by our defeat, nor by the emergence of the young fast bowler Rodney Hogg. I knew he was around because I have a lot of friends in Australia who keep me posted about likely young players and his name had cropped up. Hogg steamed in at a fair pace, took six wickets for 73 in the match and left a real impression – not least on Clive Radley's skull.

Clive was looking to play forward in the first innings when a delivery from Hogg took off from just short of a length and smacked him on the forehead with a sickening crunch, Clive reeled about, stepped on his wicket; there was blood all over the place and the wound eventually needed eight stitches.

Many people had said Clive would struggle against the extra pace and bounce in Australia and I suppose his injury seemed to support that theory. But I was at the other end and there really wasn't a great deal he could have done to avoid the ball, in fact he did well to turn his head and avoid being hit full in the face. Other front-foot players have done well in Australia – Brian Luckhurst for instance – and Clive is a good enough pro to work out the problems for himself.

But I would not have let him bat at three in the second innings. There is a school of thought that when a batsman has been hit on the head it is better to get him into the middle again as soon as possible so that his nerve doesn't go. I think Clive himself wanted to bat at three. But a blow on the head is a tremendous psychological shock and I think it was a mistake to let him bat again so soon.

Had Clive been given an extra night's rest he would have done himself more justice. The spinners might have been on, giving him a couple of overs to pick up his confidence before they brought a quickie back, as they were bound to do, and the ball would have been that much older. As it was he looked very nervous, tried to score off every delivery and was caught at square cover for three playing an awful shot. He was trying too hard and I felt sorry for him.

Hogg got me out twice in the match, which caused something of a stir. There wasn't much doubt about my lbw in the first innings; the ball pitched about off stump, kept low and would have hit middle if it hadn't hit my shin first. But I reckon I was unlucky in the second innings, given lbw to a delivery which I am sure would have missed leg stump. It was a straight ball which pitched leg and middle and hit the outside of my left knee as I shaped to play to the on-side. The Australians call that kind of decision a 'roughie', but that's the way it goes.

Hogg looked a useful prospect, strong and not too tall,

powerful across the shoulders and hips. A bit like Fred, which is a fair recommendation for any fast bowler. There might just be a question against his staying power because he has a history of asthma, but he is certainly built to last.

I was quite pleased with my batting considering it was my first match and I was bothered by a knee injury. It developed a couple of days before when we had practice in the middle and I batted in crepe soles; my back foot slipped a little when I tried to drive the spinners and I must have tweaked a ligament under my left knee.

It was pretty sore and the longer the match went on the more conscious I became of it. If I played well forward or had to turn sharply in the field I felt a stabbing pain; it became more and more difficult to concentrate. But I could have done with a longer knock in the second innings because I am the sort of player who needs runs on the board to develop rhythm and confidence; I could have done with a longer look at Hogg in case he played in the Test matches.

Beaten or not, we certainly learned one or two valuable lessons. I was very impressed with South Australia's young leg-spinner Peter Sleep, who certainly has it in him to become an Australia star in the future. He is only twenty-one but he bowled thoughtfully and didn't give anyone much to hit; reminiscent of Richie Benaud at that age.

The Australians were looking for a good performance from Rick Darling, the twenty-one-year-old right-hand batsman expected to open for them in the Tests. It was the first time I had seen him and I didn't rate his performance very highly.

Darling is a compulsive hooker and the fact that we knew it didn't seem to deter him one bit. We put men out in catching positions for the hook in each innings and he still had a go; Miller caught him off Willis for 17 in the first innings and Edmonds caught him off Old for 1 in the second. It was an obvious trap and he fell into it easily enough to make one wonder if his temperament is sufficiently developed for Test matches; he certainly has ability but self-discipline is important too. He will have to sort himself out mentally if he is going to do well in Test cricket.

The other South Australian opener John Nash gave us a

nasty shock by making a century in the first innings and 33 in the second. He looked a good, well-adjusted player but he also highlighted a tactical error which should have been spotted and rectified sooner. It is foolish to bowl for long periods in Australia without a third man.

When bowlers attack the off stump they are always likely to drop a bit short or push the ball a bit wider than they intended. In England a batsman would smack it square, wide of point's right hand; in Australia they like to back cut between point and gully or even finer. Nash played the shot a lot and exploited our lack of a third man. He got one or two edges but I suspect that about half his runs off the faster bowlers came from a deliberate shot into the third-man area. We should have been alive to that; it showed if nothing else that we had to start thinking Australian. These are the sort of wrinkles and details which become so important in Test matches.

David Gower scored 73 in the first innings and 50 in the second, the kind of start to a tour which I thought would do his confidence a tremendous amount of good; but his second innings was much the better of the two.

David gave the bowlers apoplexy in the first innings, flashing outside the off stump, edging wide of the slips, offering chances which were put down. I lost count of the number of air shots he played and the language from the bowlers at my end was unrepeatable. But he was relatively new to Australian conditions and it was good to see how he began to size up the situation in his second innings. He refused to cut out his best shots on the off-side, which was perfectly right, but he was tighter, more controlled and more selective.

Phil Edmonds bowled exceptionally well – as he usually does these days – and the match gave us the opportunity to try an experiment with Geoff Miller's offspin which seemed to work pretty smoothly. Certainly, the Aussies didn't like it which must be a strong point in its favour.

Geoff bowled to a 6–3 field, attacking the stumps around middle and forcing the batsmen to play on the on-side. Mike Brearley positioned himself at short mid-on to inhibit the drive, which is a very English fielding position and one which the Aussies rarely see and don't like. That sort of strategy demands a high degree of accuracy from the bowlers, but both Geoff and John Emburey had worked hard in the nets, getting very close to the stumps at delivery with the arm coming over about middle stump.

It says a lot for Geoff's accuracy that he bowled quite a number of his overs without a slip and his match figures of 34.4 eight-ball overs for 78 runs and five wickets speaks for itself. A very useful theory to take into the Tests.

By a wry coincidence one of the umpires in the South Australia match was Max O'Connell, who gave me run-out way back in 1971 when the bat slipped (I think that is the expression) from my hands. We had a chat, friendly enough, and neither of us mentioned the incident. It's probably better that way.

We lost the match, the local lads went wild, which wasn't surprising considering it was only their first victory in three seasons and the last time South Australia beat an English touring team was way back in 1925. But it probably did us more good than harm.

Mike called us together in the dressing room and said: 'If anyone thought this tour was going to be easy, they know now that it certainly won't be. We didn't play well but I have nothing more to say at this stage.' He didn't have to add a word.

3 Contrasting Captains

Injuries are the worst occupational hazard of a professional sportsman's life, and injuries on an Ashes tour are the last word in frustration. Bad form you can fight against, work in the nets, practise and practise until the trouble sorts itself out. But injuries take their own time. And there is a natural conflict between the desire to play and the need to rest; a fine line between the sort of exercise which speeds a cure and that which delays recovery. You are afraid of doing too much and frustrated by doing so little.

Injuries depress me because I need to have a bat in my hand. I need to practise, to develop and maintain rhythm; I soon get rusty without it. So I was particularly fed up when my knee was slow to respond to treatment and I missed the one-day match at Leongatha and, more important, the four-day game against Victoria in Melbourne.

In fact, I wasn't pencilled in to play against Victoria because it was selection policy to give everybody match practice on the early part of the tour, and that meant we were all expected to miss at least one of the four State matches before the first Test. I can see the reasoning behind that policy but I cannot pretend to agree with it.

I think England were worried by their experience in Pakistan the previous winter, when young Mike Gatting was pitched into the last Test with very little match preparation. Not surprisingly he wasn't a great success – and the selectors did not want a similar situation to arise in Australia.

Fair enough, but the circumstances on the Ashes tour were rather different and I think England should have had a flexible selection policy to recognise the fact. Mike missed out in Pakistan because there were only three-day matches before the first Test and one of those was ruined by the weather. It was genuinely difficult to give everybody a game.

In Australia we had four four-day matches and four one-day games before the first Test – enough cricket, I would have thought, to give everyone some cricket without ignoring special needs. I still think that those players who are considered to be certain to take part in the first Test should be allowed to play in every warm-up match if they want to. Otherwise you can arrive at a situation where key players are not quite in form, where everybody is eighty-five per cent ready and nobody feels absolutely prepared and confident. That is no way to go into a Test match.

If England expected Bob Taylor to keep wicket in the first Test I did not think there was any point in leaving him out of any State matches, assuming of course that he felt the need to play. Geoff Miller should have been given precedence over John Emburey for the same reason. And if Geoff Boycott was to play in the first Test he should be given as much match practice in the State games as he felt he needed. That is not selfishness; it is common sense.

Of all the Australian Test grounds, Melbourne is the one I like least. Perhaps that is partly because it doesn't seem to like me – I have never scored a century there – but probably because it is such a vast, cold, concrete place. I'm sure it was a marvellous place to be in 1956 when Kuts and Brasher were running into Olympic history, but to me it seems to have very little atmosphere for cricket.

The weather in Melbourne is the most unpredictable in Australia, the sort of place where your sunshade doubles up as an umbrella. It was cold and raining when we arrived and in fact we lost the third day completely because of rain, so what might have been a significant match was badly devalued. Victoria included likely Test players in Hurst, Callan, Higgs, Laughlin and Yallop, who was already being tipped as the Australian captain. The State side is run by Frank Tyson, still looking fit and prosperous, and is regarded as one of the more go-ahead clubs; they organised a coaching exhibition before the match and let in 13,000 schoolchildren free on the first day – a good PR exercise aimed partly at counteracting Packer, who gave free admission to kids last year. Well, it was one way of making sure they came to the ground!

The outfield was vast, lush and very slow and the pitch – covered by an inflated tent – was dry, brown and grassless. It would have more grass on it by the time we played the third Test at the end of December but for the State match it was slow and featureless, the sort of pitch where batsmen could stay in without too much trouble but wouldn't score runs very quickly.

Victoria batted after winning the toss and, inevitably, England soon had the spinners on. There was nothing in it for the quicks. Phil Edmonds bowled to the high standard which we all expect of him now, but I was particularly impressed with John Emburey, who maintained marvellous control and strangled the batsmen with unfailing accuracy – the hallmark of a class spinner when the ball refuses to turn. Victoria became frustrated and helped to get themselves out; none of their batsmen looked particularly impressive.

Hurst bowled at a lively pace despite the slow pitch and suggested he would be a pretty awkward proposition with a little help from the pitch, but Callan tried too hard to catch the selectors' eye. He bowled too many would-be bouncers on a pitch which simply would not bounce, lost his rhythm and became frustrated. The most economical of Victoria's bowlers was the legspinner Jim Higgs, but I was astounded to read that Tyson compared him favourably with Richie Benaud. He bowled tidily and accurately but I didn't think his performance was anything to write home about.

Our assistant tour manager Kenny Barrington may be just a shade long in the tooth for a return to Test cricket but he watched Higgs carefully and adopted his style of bringing the arm from behind his body which screens the ball until very late. It certainly made Kenny a better bowler in the nets; now if only someone could come up with the elixir of youth …

Derek Randall returned to the scene of his amazing 174 in the Centenary Test and made a typically attractive 62 before he became a bit too cocky, skipped down the wicket to the off-spinner Wiener and yorked himself. Derek's attitude was just right. He was under pressure to make runs and justify a Test place but he didn't let it stifle his natural game. 'I don't think I'll get in the Test side anyway so I'm going to play my shots,' he told me before the match. That's the only way he can do himself justice; it wouldn't work for every player in the side but it is clearly the best approach for him.

Mike Brearley needed a long innings and a big innings to bolster his confidence – 116 not out in seven hours seventeen minutes should certainly have helped! The crowd didn't exactly appreciate it, in fact I heard one spectator demanding that Brearley should get out and let me take his place, but I can only assume he was joking!

To be fair to Mike, the outfield was dreadfully slow and many shots which should have run for four were picked up in the lush grass for two. He was not in the best of form and his innings should have done him and England a lot of good. Mike is not the most exhilarating of strokeplayers at the best of times, but he stuck to his job with real determination, picking up most of his runs off his legs through midwicket or behind square.

Yallop's captaincy was interesting but surprising. He was under pressure, of course, not least because the week before he put Queensland in to bat and lost the match, which brought him quite a lot of stick from the critics. Strange how a captain can take so much hammer when things go wrong, as if ten other players weren't involved in defeat, when in the past indifferent players leading ten very good ones to victory have been acclaimed as great skippers.

Yallop didn't look very imaginative in the State game. He allowed Higgs to bowl without fielders close to the bat, which took a considerable amount of pressure off the batsmen, and he seemed reluctant to experiment with bowling changes even when the ball was hitting the middle of the bat with repetitive monotony. Higgs bowled long, unsuccessful spells when a bowling change or simply a change of ends might have brought a breakthrough.

Captains cannot work miracles but above all they have to be imaginative, and my impression after the State game was that if Yallop captained Australia, we would have a head start playing under Brearley. That could become a very important factor.

My involvement in the match was restricted to a couple of appearances as drinks waiter. Apart from that I rested my knee, had treatment and tried it out gingerly in the nets – still not very happy with the way it was going. There was improvement but it was only slow, and all the time there was this nagging psychological problem, restrictive and inhibiting.

That was why I was anxious to play in the one-day match at Canberra. Knee or no knee, I simply had to have match practice with the days ticking away to the first Test. As it turned out, the practice was very useful.

I did not play in the first two one-day games but I gather they were of limited usefulness. The match against South Australian Country at Renmark was drawn and England won the game against Victoria Country at Leongatha.

None of the players who took part in it is likely to forget Renmark, the first match of the tour – even after they have forgotten the game itself! After all, it's not every day your aircraft has to circle while the groundstaff chase kangaroos off the runway. Renmark means red mud, which summed up the airstrip and the pitch. It was a desperately slow pitch and we could not bowl them out after Clive Radley had made 64 in a total of 199–4 declared. The team's plane groped after the tail lights of a station wagon to find the runway for the return trip and took off along an avenue of flickering flares. Quite a day.

Leongatha means Low Hanging Cloud – about zero height when England played. The weather was atrocious and the match would not have been played had it been first class. But everyone for miles around had turned out to see England so the lads decided they would give it a go. Just after lunch there was a torrential downpour and several players took the field with their trousers tucked into their socks; John Emburey bowled them out and England won in the last over. It was a fine public relations exercise and I think the locals really appreciated it.

Canberra is a beautiful city, a striking example of what can be done when planners start from scratch with time, money and unlimited space to express themselves. It covers a huge area without sprawling, full of attractive buildings, parks and fountains. It is quite possible to walk through a semi-residential area and feel you are deep in the country, along tree-lined roads and amid well-kept lawns. The legations and embassies are all built in a beautifully distinctive style and set in spacious grounds, screened from the road by shrubs and trees, shimmering white or – like the Japanese and Thai embassies – fashioned in magnificent pagoda style. I fancied a round of golf on the Royal Canberra course, which looks as though it was laid out by Capability Brown and tended by Percy Thrower, but work comes first.

It was a beautifully sunny day at the opulent cricket ground, which meant we were fortunate because it had been snowing only a few days before we arrived. The Australia Capital Territories team were about Minor Counties standard with one or two players perhaps a little better, but they were very keen, anxious not to let themselves down.

We won the match easily after I scored 123 not out, Roger Tolchard made 108 and then Bob Willis whipped up a fair pace which left the local lads a bit bewildered. They were 15–5 at one stage and lost by 179 runs.

The pitch was pretty lively early on, I was a bit rusty for the first hour and Graham Gooch was caught behind off their best bowler, a medium-pacer called Horneman. But I felt I was playing quite freely by the end, timing the square and back cuts smoothly.

Tolly and I put on 229 for the second wicket and I must say he looked in tremendous form. He is particularly good against spinners, using his feet and improvising, and he runs superbly between the wickets. I enjoyed that because it made the whole innings pacey and exhilarating; it's great fun to bat with a quick runner.

I reckon about 200 of the partnership were all-run, which is quite a distance when you calculate it as twenty-yard sprints. I was pretty tired at the end and no wonder, but at least my knee stood up to it pretty well. As the old man of the team I was positioned at leg slip when the ACT side batted and I picked up two catches, one each off Bob Willis and Mike Hendrick.

There was a fair amount of gentle mickey-taking at that.

After the catch off Willis, John Lever ran in all the way from fine leg and called out: 'Lovely catch, well taken, Embers.' When I protested that I had taken it everybody fell about in convulsions. Hendo elected me as his regular leg slip after my second catch, so honour was satisfied ...

4 Botham signs in

When November 17th dawned the England camp breathed a huge sigh of relief. Ian Botham was finally passed fit to play against New South Wales in Sydney, his first match on tour following an injury to his left wrist just before we left England. Ian had suffered agonies of frustration for a month and we had endured all the practical jokes and rib-crushing pranks of a young giant with unlimited energy and little opportunity to burn it off.

Tangling with Ian in a playful mood is like wrestling a grizzly – and he was absolutely determined to be playful. Clive Radley fled whenever 'Both' appeared, which showed a healthy streak of self-preservation, but there isn't much you can do when you find your socks full of melting ice cubes and a certain member of the team is sitting whistling innocently in the corner. I left my best bat in the dressing room in Melbourne and discovered that all the Victoria team had autographed it for me; strange how they all wrote just like Ian Botham...

He had been champing at the bit ever since we arrived. 'Better be awake at fine leg when I get going, Fiery; there will be a few top edges flying about,' he promised. We didn't expect too much from him in terms of performance – after all, he had not played for two months – but being Both, he surprised us all. Bill O'Reilly, old Tiger himself, helped us out quite a bit.

Rusty or not, Ian belted his first ball in Australia for four and made 56 out of a first-innings total of 374. He looked remarkably good, especially against the spinners, and NSW made a tactical error in not bringing back their fastest bowler, Geoff Lawson, when the new ball was available. Lawson had him in quite a bit of trouble next day and O'Reilly wrote in a local newspaper that he didn't think this chap Botham would give Australia much trouble in the series. That was all Ian needed.

He had not bowled particularly well in the first innings but his own combatitiveness – and O'Reilly's remarks – provided the proverbial red rag to a Somerset bull. He took the new ball, finished with five wickets in a ten-wicket victory and bowled especially well against their best batsman, Peter Toohey. A vote of thanks to Mr O'Reilly.

Sydney is my favourite Australian city, full of life and bounce, within easy reach of superb beaches and with its own quiet nooks and crannies. I know it fairly well after playing with a local club Waverley a couple of years ago.

The team's hotel was situated on the edge of King's Cross, which is to Sydney today what Soho was to London twenty years ago. The women must be very tired because quite a lot of them lounge in shop doorways and lean against buildings in the street. They often ask if you are interested in business, so I suppose it must be the commercial centre of the city; I never found out for sure.

We had been on tour for over three weeks. I felt desperately out of touch. I had had only three innings, including the one-day at Canberra, and that for me is hopelessly little cricket. When I got a bat in my hand out in the middle it felt as though I was starting the tour all over again; there had been very little continuity and that always hits me hard.

I felt I had played well after the first hour at Canberra, but I was also disturbed that it took me so long to get going, especially since the bowling in a State match would be far tighter and more demanding than in the district game. Practice was the only answer but the nets, most unusually for Sydney, were very poor.

We could not risk facing our bowlers firing it in off a full run. They had to cut down to a steady pace and pitch the ball up, which is exactly what we did not need in terms of meaningful practice. The new ball in Australia comes through at an alarming pace, it is vital that batsmen – and especially those high in the order – accustom themselves to extra pace and bounce simply in the interests of survival. From that point of view, the nets were all but useless.

Lawson is a pretty torrid customer. I had heard about him from friends in Aussie who described him as 'pretty slippery', which is their way of saying he could be decidedly nasty. They know a bowler when they see one and they don't exaggerate. I batted for fifty-one minutes against Lawson and Watson, who can move the ball about quite appreciably, and I felt I had done most of the hard work when Lawson got me out. He let one go early, bowled it from twenty-three yards in fact, and I got there a little too early, pushed away from my body and gave an easy catch to slip.

Lawson was not picked in the first Test squad but he looked on the fringe of being selected. The biggest mark against him is his stamina; he did not bowl long spells and never looked too happy coming back after his initial burst, still troublesome but not as quick. At twenty-one, he still has time to broaden and develop bowling strength.

Graham Gooch made 66 but, like the rest of use, he still looked as though he needed more cricket to sharpen him up. He played and missed quite a bit against Watson and didn't give the impression he was in solid form, but he treated the slower bowlers with far less respect and produced some delightful square cuts and off drives.

Derek Randall got a hundred, a headache and a telling off from Mike Brearley. He really is an incredible cricketer. Having seen how formidable Lawson could be with the new ball, Derek promptly tried to hook the second ball he received and was hit on the head. His cap flew off, Derek disappeared inside a ring of anxious fielders and we in the dressing room really feared he was badly hurt ... until he emerged grinning and clowning as though nothing had happened.

I remember when Lillee skulled him in the Centenary Test and Derek called back: 'No good hitting me there, mate; nothing to damage.' Daft as a brush, but a great individual who should not let anybody change him. He looked relaxed, played his shots boldly and enjoyed himself against Mark Clews, a right-arm seamer who did not look a very formidable proposition in the State match.

When he had made 110 Derek got himself out with a dreadfully lazy stroke, caught at cover. Mike Brearley taxed him about that the next day and Derek admitted he was feeling tired after some four hours at the crease. But the captain, quite rightly, told him that simply would not do.

Test cricket demands concentration and application not for three or four hours but for seven or eight. A batsman has to steel himself to that kind of innings for the sake of the team, because the man who is good enough or lucky enough to establish himself simply must not give it away. If a century takes four hours, the hundredth run is not a release; it's the start of another four hours' batting.

If Derek was tired – and the pressures which build in the nineties obviously take a great deal out of every batsman – then he should have taken a breather. It is possible, even in Test matches, to decide you will take it easy for twenty minutes, let your partner have most of the strike and gently allow yourself to recuperate mentally.

The alternative to that is often a great flood of relief after reaching a century, a period of relative carelessness and the sort of stroke which got Derek out. It happens all the time – look how many players are out soon after reaching a hundred – and it is a temptation which has to be overcome.

Radley looked nervous and tentative before he jabbed a catch down short leg's throat off the left-arm orthodox spinner, and David Gower played a strangely hybrid little innings – one or two golden shots mingled with some streaky ones. He was lax in not spotting David Hourn's quick topspinner, which pushed him on to the back foot, hurried through and bowled him for 26.

I saw quite a lot of Hourn during my spell with Waverley and he is a fascinating bowler, a left-arm spinner who bowls a chinaman, googly, topspinner and a speciality ball which he can keep low and hurry through at will. All difficult to spot, all difficult to play. He did not bowl particularly well against us, perhaps because he was conscious of Test possibilities and over-anxious to impress. He tried too many variations, lost his line and bowled too wide of the off stump, a liberty you cannot take with Test-class batsmen. But it was noticeable that when he did bowl accurately, nobody played him with complete confidence.

After Both's half century, we were given an unexpected

bonus by a tenth-wicket stand of 38 between Bob Willis and Mike Hendrick. And what a revelation! Hendo suddenly began playing as though he had never batted lower than five in his life, cover-driving along the ground with a fine, full swing of the bat, and Bob took his cue from that. NSW could hardly believe it, we weren't quite sure what was going on and I suspect that Messrs Hendrick and Willis weren't altogether certain themselves.

But the fact is that their partnership was the sort of bonus we could not expect in a Test Match. Only three batsmen – Randall, Gooch and Botham – had made solid scores in a total of 374 and they had got themselves out when they were well established. There was a lesson to be learned from that – simply that Test batting requires any batsman who has established himself to go on and on. It is so easy to lose wickets early to the new ball that those who do get in have to make it count.

Again, I had reservations about the way in which the State captain Andrew Hilditch handled the bowling attack. Lawson had bowled only six overs in the morning session and in my view should have been pretty well rested, yet he was not recalled immediately after lunch and in fact returned only after Gooch and Randall had faced several overs of spin and medium pace. The ball was still fairly new and I thought NSW should have been looking for Lawson to strike a wicket or two. Nor was he brought on immediately when Botham went in, which also seemed like a bad tactical error to me.

We were interested to see what Peter Toohey was made of. He has emerged as the pin-up boy of Australian batsmen after so many departures to WSC and had a high reputation as a player; in fact there was a good deal of speculation that Packer might jump in and recruit him before the series started.

It quickly became obvious that Toohey likes to get on the front foot and drive, especially through the off-side. So it wasn't long before Hendo was bowling to a 7–2 field with a fine leg and straightish mid-on, bowling just outside off stump and challenging Toohey to drive. That was tempting his strength but it also meant he had to time his shot perfectly – we had four slips and two gullies in case he made a mistake – and of course he was conscious of this.

Toohey clipped Hendo off his legs when his line strayed and produced a couple of nice off drives but he eventually became irritated, tried to hit over cover off the back foot – which is one of the most difficult shots in the game – and was caught by David Gower. A fine piece of bowling and a shrewd tactical victory for the team; it should have given Toohey something to think about.

Bob Willis also bowled with exemplary control and accuracy to an attacking field, but the biggest success of the innings was Geoff Miller, who maintained a very good line and finished with six wickets. It was especially important for Geoff to do well because he hasn't taken many Test wickets and he did not bowl too well in the home series last season. Yet he is regarded as a genuine Test all-rounder in the making and I know Mike Brearley was keen to see him develop that way.

Both Miller and Emburey employed our leg-side theory, NSW did not look as though they could make much of it and even their most determined batsman Dyson finally became frustrated and tried to hit over the top. Unfortunately for him there was an athletic young man in the area who raced round, dived, tumbled and rolled, smacked his head on the ground and still held the ball aloft in one hand. His name is in the scorebook ... !

The State side collapsed to 165 and there was some discussion as to whether we ought to enforce the follow-on or give our batsmen more practice. Much as our batsmen needed match practice, we felt it was important to win well if we could – this was, after all, a prestigious State match. The result of a lesser match might not have mattered so much.

So we put them back in, Botham took umbrage at Tiger O'Reilly's remarks and we bowled them out again for 210. Toohey was out for 20 and Both did the damage this time, bowling the line for Toohey's favourite off-side shots but not the length to enable him to play with safety. Eventually he tried to drive a good-length ball, partly in frustration, and nicked it to Graham Gooch at slip.

Hilditch tried hard to save it and I would have been inclined to take the new ball earlier, especially since the spinners bowled for most of the afternoon without much joy. As it was, the new ball was taken after tea and NSW were soon rolled over. Botham finished their innings with a straight full toss and then flung his arms high above his head in a gesture to the Press box ...

The match was as good as over – we needed only two to win – but there was still a bit of drama to come. I knew that if we sent in our regular openers they would face a pretty torrid few minutes because NSW had absolutely nothing to lose and Lawson still fancied making a name for himself, particularly against me. Still, duty calls – and Lawson let me have three consecutive bouncers before umpire Tom Brooks warned him for persistent intimidation. As bouncers go they weren't much to write home about; I got out of the way easily enough. But that did not prevent the Press from making a big thing out of it, Bumper Wars and all that. No wonder people always seemed to associate Boycott with controversy.

After he had been warned and the captain had spoken to him, Lawson let one go just short of a length which got up awkwardly, hit me on the wrist and looped over slip for the winning runs. Tom Brooks regarded it as a challenge to his authority and was pretty annoyed about it, though there was little he could do since the match was over.

Five minutes at the crease hardly counts as an innings so I still felt short of match practice at the end of the NSW game. I did not play in the up-country match at Bundaberg which England won by 132 runs, and I suspect a certain Scott Ledger wishes he had not played either. He retired hurt after being hit by John Lever, returned much later in the order and promptly retired hurt again after being hit by his first ball! I suppose you could call that one for the book.

What made it worse was that Ledger was simply acting under instructions. When he went in for the second time Derek Randall offered a bit of advice from the depth of his experience: 'For heaven's sake, mate, if you get one short of a length don't be trying to hook, just play safe and duck,' said Derek. The first ball was short and Ledger ducked into it ...

Winning matches convincingly is a good habit but it does increase the problems of match practice before the first Test.

Perhaps when future tours are planned the itinerary could include more one-day matches, preferably without the travelling involved at present. It is a very important PR exercise to take cricket into the districts and there is no doubt it is very popular; we are always handsomely treated. I am sure it is a difficult problem for the ruling bodies but perhaps the district teams could also travel to meet the tourists and more matches could be arranged that way.

5   Bouncers and blood

Sooner or later we were bound to be involved in some sort of
bouncer controversy. It seems to be part of the Australian tour
scene, a source of morbid fascination for spectators and a newsy
talking point for the Press. Like any war, a so-called bouncer
war always seems to intrigue and attract those who are not
actually involved in it.

The pitches in Brisbane and Perth are traditionally the
quickest in Australia and, more than that, they are notorious
for their extravagant bounce. Playing there can be rather like
playing on concrete with a golf ball; not a very bright prospect
for batsmen, though high scores have been made at both
grounds over the years.

Like most touring teams before us, we practised at the
church school in Brisbane, where the headmaster is a former
Cambridge blue and the facilities are absolutely first class. It
was a sobering experience for some who had never met such
fast, bouncy pitches before. We simply dared not give the
quicker bowlers a new ball to use in the nets. It goes through
like a bullet, bounces a foot or more higher than it would at
home and, being new, can cut dramatically off the pitch. So
unless you actually like being sawn in two about chest high
there is no real advantage to be gained from practising against
the new ball. Everybody was in trouble of some sort but we had
to get in as much net practice as possible to prepare us for the
State match and the Test, which was only a week or so away.

I have always believed that a combination of high pace and
exceptional bounce is bad for the game of cricket, and pitches
which encourage both do a disservice to players and spectators
alike. Speed alone is a legitimate problem which batsmen can
overcome if they have the proper technique: if a player gets in

42

line he has ball sense and reflexes to combat the quickest delivery.

But what happens to the batsman who gets into line and then finds that the ball just short of a length is bouncing not chest high but throat and mouth high? He cannot get out of line – there's not a lot of time when the ball is coming through like a train – and if he is lucky he manages to glove the ball to gully or fend it off the splice to short leg.

So the thinking batsman deliberately avoids getting in line. The Aussies, who are far more used to this situation than we are, tend to step away and slash the rising ball over gully and slip. A sensible enough strategy but obviously bad technique to anyone who is taught, as English players are from a very early age, that it is important to get in line.

If getting in line is good technique for twelve-, sixteen- and twenty-year-olds, why should it become bad practice in Australian Shield or Test cricket? I consider any pitch which destroys fundamentals rather than testing them must be bad for the game.

I practised as long and as often as I could; I got in line because I do not know any other way to play. But at the back of my mind there was always the tactical dilemma of whether to stay in line or keep slightly away from the ball. Decide to stay in line and run the risk of giving away a wicket in self-defence; play slightly away from the ball and edge a catch off some innocuous medium-pacer? A difficult situation.

And imagine our reaction when we discovered that the pitch on which we would play the State game was a relatively make-shift job. The groundsman decided at the last minute that the pitch he had prepared might not last a full four days so he cut a new strip alongside, the same one on which Australia had beaten India convincingly – thanks largely to their seamers – a year ago. The thought of playing on a fast, bouncy pitch which was under-prepared cheered us all up no end, and I wasn't exactly upset when Queensland won the toss and decided to bat.

The first ball from Bob Willis said it all. It wasn't particularly short and it wasn't especially quick, a loosener which he dug in quite hard but no more. It took off, cleared the batsman and Bob Taylor by three feet and ran down to the sightscreen for four byes!

By lunch we had dropped three catches, had one disallowed, taken one wicket and conceded 86 runs – an eventful start but not one we were particularly pleased with. Bob Willis was upset when the opening batsman Broad flashed at him and we reckoned he was caught behind off bottom edge; but the umpire gave him not out. Everybody near the bat was edgy, and there were a few hard words flying around.

To make matters worse Broad had already been dropped by Graham Gooch at long leg and later Ogilvie was dropped twice – first by Bob Taylor, which doesn't happen too often, and then by Mike Brearley at first slip. A ragged sort of morning for us.

It came right in the afternoon – Queensland lost nine wickets in doubling their score – but I confess I did not enjoy it much as a game of cricket. Some of Willis's early stuff was quite frightening, whistling through head-high from just short of a length; batsmen played and missed, slashed and nicked the ball, ducked and weaved. It might have been exciting from a spectator's point of view but I don't think it represented cricket as it is meant to be played.

Ogilvie eventually ducked into a short-pitched delivery from Willis, realised he could not avoid it completely and fortunately managed to turn his face away before it smacked him at the side of the head. He went down on his knees with blood streaming down his neck and tottered off to be stitched up.

The Queenslanders' technique against the bouncing ball was interesting. No question of getting in line, they simply stood back and slashed hard or got inside the line and hooked. Anything inside their half was an invitation to drive very fiercely, not just half volleys but anything remotely near a full length.

Gary Cosier was a very good example of this. If the ball was pitched up he had a go, not too concerned if it went in the air just so long as it was safe. Strong and aggressive, a real slogger of the ball – and he played one shot off Chris Old which was absolutely magnificent. Old dropped one a bit short and Cosier flipped it off his hip high and far over the long-leg boundary: a great shot!

Call me conservative if you like, but I still think there's more to cricket than hooking and ducking. If batsmen have to frame an innings with the fear of being hit lurking at the back of their minds, the game loses a great deal of its charm and attractiveness. It loses half its strokes for a start and that, surely, is bad for the game. Queensland were dismissed for 172, we naturally had the heavy roller on and it took me eighteen minutes to enrich the Queensland lads by $1,000.

A local businessman had offered the team that much if they could get me out for under 20. I am not generally philanthropic when it comes to getting out but I was surprised by a delivery from the medium-pacer Brabon which bounced a little and hurried off the pitch, caught at slip by Cosier for 6.

Brabon had bowled at me before, though I didn't remember it at the time. While I was with Waverley in 1977 I went coaching to Rockhampton and he was among those who bowled at me in the nets. He might even have got me out then, but as far as I recall nobody gave him $1,000 for doing it.

Our batting still did not look too healthy considering it was the last match before the Test, but fortunately Derek Randall continued his run of good form, Graham Gooch made 34 after being dropped twice hooking, and Mike Brearley weighed in with a determined 75 not out. Randall was in such good form that he played a most unusual shot with confidence – hooking high and handsomely backward of square leg from outside the line of the ball! Considering the uncertain nature of the pitch he played really well.

Mike's innings was sound rather than spectacular, which was no bad thing when we needed players in form. He had to duck and weave early on but by the time he reached 50 he was timing the ball nicely and produced some handsome shots. He and Derek were the only batsmen with any real form to speak of and we could have done with a long innings from Geoff Miller, but he received a superb delivery from Dymock which pitched and left him when he had made 18 and was caught behind. Still, Geoff himself felt a lot happier with his performance and confidence means a great deal.

We made 254, which gave us a lead of 82, and Bob Willis quickly had Queensland in real trouble with two wickets in his first over. Broad was given out lbw and there were some eye-brows raised because he hesitated. I imagine he thought the ball might just have been missing leg stump and in any case I don't think it is up to batsmen to give themselves out. If there is a doubt I think a batsman is entitled to wait and see; decisions go against them often enough.

Soon afterwards Queensland lost their third wicket in near-tragic circumstances. Their opener, Max Walters, looked desperately uneasy: he was on a pair and he obviously did not relish the quicker stuff on this pitch. He was fidgeting and nervous, the sort of player who invites a bouncer. Willis dug one in just short of a length – not a bouncer but nasty enough on this pitch.

It took off, Walters played back in alarm and the ball smacked him sickeningly straight between the eyes. There was blood everywhere and the horror we all felt was increased because Walters plays in spectacles; it was a dreadful moment. Mike Brearley began to dash forward from slip and then turned back momentarily to compose himself while Walters doubled up on his knees in the crease.

The bridge of his spectacles had been forced into his nose but fortunately the glasses themselves had spun off without breaking. Walters was helped off the field and took no further part in the game; goodness knows, nobody blamed him.

Bob Willis didn't say anything – few fast bowlers do in situations like that – but I think he was a bit shaken. He pitched the ball well up and was driven by Carlson and the left-hander Hohns, conceding more runs than he ought because we did not have a mid-off or mid-on. Tactically I would have bowled Bob and Chris Old a little less: both batsmen were going quite well and Hohns was given far too many cheap runs off his legs.

Ian Botham came on forty minutes before the close and snatched a couple of wickets – it's incredible how often he does something like that – and we should have finished Queensland off next day. But Ogilvie came back wearing a crash helmet; Hohns played his shots with the help of some pretty loose stuff down the leg side and the fifth wicket put on a frustrating thirty-eight runs. That was the shape of things to come.

The match drifted away from us as we were made to work desperately hard to get through the tail. Maclean clung on and on, surviving a half chance to Phil Edmonds at backward short leg off Geoff Miller, Edmonds himself finally bowled a bouncer in frustration and Botham appealed for a fanciful lbw against Maclean, cupping his hands with a huge grin and adding 'Please ...' But Maclean was running out of partners, especially since Walters would be little more than nuisance value, and he finally took a swipe at Old and was caught by Gooch running in from the third-man boundary for 94.

We needed 208 to win when at one stage we had been looking forward to a day off, but I suppose the practice was more useful than the rest. Gooch and Balcam had a bit of a set-to, a flurry of bouncers and an exchange of words in the middle. Balcam took the mickey, mimicking Graham, but Carlson took his wicket when he edged a catch to gully.

The team were anxious about the lack of runs coming from Graham, David Gower and me and I was still dissatisfied with my own form. I struggled to find any sort of rhythm at first and simply concentrated on surviving into the following day. I was edgy, ill at ease and generally a bit late with my shots. Ian Botham put a fatherly paw on my shoulder and said: 'Just stay at the wicket, Fiery; it'll come', and by the time I was caught down the leg-side for 60 I felt better for four hours at the crease. But it was still not right, still not positive and decisive enough. I felt I was judging deliveries well but there was still a block; I still felt very tentative about playing forward on to my left knee.

Derek Randall looked in super form again, as chirpy and cheeky as ever. He got himself out, driving over a straight one, but not before he had informed short square leg, 'Wouldn't stand there to me if I was you. Get yourself killed, y'know.' Derek has also taken to singing at the wicket ...

Mike Brearley looked really confident and positive in the second innings. He was not afraid to whack the offspinner Whyte uppishly through mid-on and then lift him over mid-wicket for four. 'That's just a bloody slog,' said Whyte – and Mike was offended enough to play a beautiful square cut-drive off the face of the bat for four more. Balcam made him skip about a bit with a few bouncers near the end but Mike survived, 38 not out.

Geoff Miller needed practice in the middle and made a good-looking 22 not out, but David Gower – who needed runs just as badly – tried to drive the legspinner Hohns square on the off-side and was caught at slip. A six-wicket win was convincing enough on paper but we knew we still had problems.

6 Australia collapse

I might never have played in the first Test match and had that been the case, a young blond Aussie by the name of Carl Whatsisname would have become an overnight sensation. I cannot remember Carl's full name but he was a striking figure, tall and built like an Adonis, who bowled at us in the nets at the Church school. Two deliveries one afternoon put me close to hospital and Carl close to instant fame or notoriety.

They lifted, hurried through and smacked off my gloves a few inches in front of my face while I took whatever evasive action I could to preserve my dignity, my teeth and my nose. We ducked and weaved our way towards December 1st at the Gabba.

Training and practice were intense, but at least partly informal; we could do fitness training in shorts and bare backs but the management were keen that net practices were undertaken in whites. That's a good thing, it keeps the atmosphere professional and valuable. The bouncy nets saw to it that we didn't relax too much; I picked out a green, English-looking tree and told the schoolboys they should bury me there if the worst came to the worst ...

There was, of course, a more serious side to the levity. I think everybody was aware of the problem and possibility of bouncers and Roger Tolchard arranged for a helmet salesman to come round a couple of days before the Test started. Several players invested in a helmet at $25 a time, green for the Aussies and blue for England. They looked more like caps than crash helmets except that they incorporated plastic protection for the side of the head; I didn't feel the need for one so I didn't buy one, but Bob Taylor, David Gower, Ian Botham, Geoff Miller and Chris Old wore them during the Test. £15 isn't a very high price to put on a skull.

Mike Brearley and Graham Yallop met and thrashed out a common policy on bouncers, a good idea after the incident at Edgbaston last year when Bob Willis felled the Pakistan nightwatchman Qasim and sparked off a row about who was and was not a recognised batsman. Apart from Bob Willis and Jim Higgs, who carry a bat for decoration rather than as a useful weapon, nobody was to be immune from bouncers. Tail-enders could expect a certain amount of consideration but if they stayed around long enough to be a nuisance they could expect to be bounced like everybody else – and nightwatchmen were definitely 'recognised' batsmen.

Packer's first night match in Sydney had pulled in around 45,000 spectators and some 20,000 had turned up at a daylight WSC match soon after, so I expected there would be comparisons between the pulling power of the two series. The Press were after me for comment but I referred them to the manager – and I got the distinct impression one or two of them were not very pleased about that. It seems the Aussie journalists expect their players to dance to all sorts of tunes and I notice Yallop was quoted as saying Australia would win all six Tests. I find it hard to believe that he really said this, but if he did he was making a rod for his own back.

Cash incentives in the Test series were considerable. Each Test was worth $9,000 – about £5,500 – in bonuses split in such a way as to encourage positive cricket. Of that, $5,000 went to the winner, $2,500 to the loser and $1,500 into a jackpot at the end of each Test. If the match was drawn, the full $9,000 went into the jackpot. At the end of the series the jackpot was to be split in half and sub-divided again.

One half of the jackpot would be equally divided and paid to the team or teams which had sustained an average overs rate of 100 balls per hour. No rate, no pay. The other half would be split two-thirds to the winner of the series and one-third to the loser. It all sounded a bit complicated but what it boiled down to was that we would be rewarded for keeping the game moving, playing positively and winning matches.

The day before the match we suffered an unexpected casualty but fortunately – though I don't suppose he saw it that way – it was only Doug Insole ... Doug was helping us out with slip catching practice, edging the ball to Bob Taylor, Derek Randall and myself off the throwing of Bob Willis. Now Bob is not ideal for that job, if only because he is not the most accurate of throwers and the ball tends to inswing a bit unpredictably even from twelve yards or so. The first throw hit Doug on the elbow, the second was slogged miles away in a fit of understandable pique – not much slip practice in that – and the third hit him in the ribs. Doug collapsed in agony while the practice squad collapsed in hysteria. The manager was always good for morale.

The team was fairly predictable. There had been some Press talk about Mike Brearley going in first but this was never discussed at team level; we were all concerned that David Gower had not played nearly as well as he could but then, as the manager said, David is a touch player, one who reacts to the big occasion. He can shrug off a poor run of form just because the situation appeals to him.

Naturally we discussed their players in some detail; in fact, I sometimes wonder if people realise just how carefully we sift through strengths and weaknesses before a Test match. When you consider how many brains are set to deceive and frustrate batsmen, it's a wonder they score any runs at all. Maclean had just made 94 for Queensland against us so we had plenty of opportunity to study him: likes to cut, keep the ball well up to him and straight, cramp his style. Hughes plays very straight off the back foot but his temperament may be vulnerable: he is always anxious to get off the mark, keep him fretting on nought for as long as possible. Yallop has been described by Alan Davidson as the best player of spin bowling in Australia; quicks against him whenever possible. Laughlin likes to hook and pull the quicker bowlers and will attack the spinners; must set a long-on for him against spin. Yardley plays his shots if the ball is pitched up and likes the square slash. Hurst and Hogg will slog the spinners and go for the seamers if the ball is pitched up. And Higgs is no batsman at all. Those were our views in outline and several of our impressions were to prove quite prophetic.

Bob Willis reminded the team meeting that anyone could receive a bouncer which, apart from being potentially dangerous, is a fiendishly difficult delivery to play well. 'If you intend to hook, then set your stall out and hook with conviction,' he said. After a salutary lesson at Wellington on the previous winter tour of New Zealand, Bob also warned the meeting against winding down too much on rest day. It is terribly difficult to build yourself up for a Test day once you have relaxed and unwound; during the first session after the rest day in Wellington we were badly out of touch in the field.

England had not won a Test match in Brisbane since 1936, but the state of the pitch insisted that just might be remedied this time. The Test strip was about three widths away from the one used for the Queensland game and had not been prepared much by the time that match finished. It had been watered and rolled a lot but on the day before the Test started it seemed to dry out and change colour. I felt that if it played like the Queensland pitch and Test bowlers got to work on it, the match would be over in four days.

First day

Skydivers representing Australia, England and the Queensland Cricket Association dropped in on the pitch, we were introduced formally to the State governor and presented with medals commemorating fifty years of cricket in Brisbane. Then Mike Brearley changed an old habit, called tails instead of heads and did us a favour by losing the toss.

Graham Yallop elected to bat and there is no doubt that England would have done the same in his shoes; several players were disappointed that we did not get the chance to bat first. But the surface was easy to scratch with a stud and the soil was black underneath and that, in my experience of Australian pitches, meant moisture. I expected it to do a bit and the weather was warm and overcast, just the conditions English bowlers like to exploit. I was not sorry we lost the toss.

Psychology plays a big part in Test cricket. The captain who puts the other side in to bat also puts pressure on his own bowlers because they feel they are expected to do well; the side that elects to bat feels it will do well because it is already in command of the situation. But Australia's psychology on that first morning, in my opinion, was all wrong.

Perhaps it was inexperience – after all, Australia had nobody in the side with the knowledge of Test cricket to warn the batsmen how difficult it might be; there was nobody to say, 'Calm down, stick around for a while.' Batsmen played their shots as though they felt that somebody would come off sooner or later. In no time at all wickets fell.

At first sight, Wood looked very fidgety for an opener. He was anxious to get off the mark – too anxious, because he soon pushed one short on the off-side and set off with Gower swooping in. Cosier is a big lad, it takes him a few strides to get up steam and he was still straining for his ground when Gower's underarm throw ran him out.

Willis produced a magnificent delivery which pitched just short of a length, swung a little and seamed back off the pitch. The gap between Toohey's bat and pad was wide enough; Australia 5–2.

Old always bowls well against left-handers and he soon had Wood in real trouble. Wood looked fairly impressive for a youngster but he obviously needed to calm himself down – and that wasn't easy with Old teasing him outside the off stump. When that had got Wood into a state of indecision, Old began to swing the ball into him and Wood had quite a different problem to contend with. Finally Old darted in a delivery which threatened to swing in but pitched and left him, Wood got an edge and Old took a wicket with a supremely Test-class piece of bowling.

Yallop was clearly trying hard to consolidate and see off the new ball, but he was in trouble against Willis and escaped when Gooch dropped him off Old. It might have been Brearley's catch at first slip but Gooch dived across from second slip and put it down. Nothing was said, it rarely is in circumstances like those; slip catchers work on the principle that if you think you can catch it – go for it. And Yallop didn't last long. Willis spun round him completely as he pushed towards midwicket area and Gooch took the catch on his knees.

Old had injured his little finger fielding in the slips and had to go off for treatment so Botham went on at the pavilion end. Inevitably – or so it seems – he took a wicket with his fourth delivery – Hughes driving and caught behind.

53

Australia were 24–5 and Hughes's shot helped to explain why. With four wickets down and the side in terrible trouble, somebody should have been fighting simply to stay there, to absorb time and give the innings time to catch its breath. Instead of that Hughes was driving on the up, a good-wicket shot on a good batsman's day!

And Laughlin ... the first time he received a short one he hooked (shades of the team talk) and Lever took a superb running catch at fine leg. Laughlin should have recognised the folly of that shot in the circumstances and thought, 'Over my dead body', but he and others before him seemed to think they were having a net. 'Let's have a go; get a few shots out of our system and then get on with the Test match ...' Australia were 26–6, not the best position to start a Test match from.

Willis bowled right through to lunch, ten eight-ball overs which was a great feat considering that *his* great feet were sore and giving him quite a lot of pain. He did not bowl flat out, quick but well within himself. Maclean and Yardley batted sensibly for half an hour or so to lunch.

Yardley was dropped by Gooch off Botham at second slip but again, it was not a costly mistake because in the next over he tried to square drive Willis and was caught behind. Maclean battled on, hooking Botham confidently for four, and Hogg helped him put on 60 for the eighth wicket in seventy-nine minutes, a frustrating time for England until Botham popped up with another piece of magic.

He had Hogg caught behind, bowling slightly wider of the crease to deceive him with the angle of the delivery and then had Hurst caught behind for a duck – two wickets in five deliveries, even if Hurst appeared to think he hadn't touched it (and I was inclined to agree with him). Higgs lasted just as long as it took Old to bowl a straight ball, which wasn't very long. And to think his wicket counts one – just like Bradman!

Australia 116 all out and I knew then that unless they took four or five wickets very quickly they had lost the first Test. On playing performance alone, it is impossible to recover after being bowled out in four hours on the first day of a five-day Test. We knew we had time and we were in no mood to let them off the hook.

Gooch was unlucky. He appeared to be three or four inches away from a delivery from Hogg which ballooned off his pad to Laughlin at gully, but all the Aussies went up for the catch and the umpire – perhaps under pressure – gave him out. Poor Graham was very disappointed.

The ball swung and seamed a bit; Hurst bowled me one magnificent delivery which pitched leg and middle and went over the off stump, but Randall and I felt we were going pretty well in seeing off the new ball.

Seeing wasn't that easy. The light faded and Randall finally said he could not pick up the ball. In Australia batsmen are allowed one appeal per session against the light so I told Randall he must make use of it. We were staggered when the umpires turned it down.

Ten minutes later the umpires took us off the field and we were taking our pads off, convinced that there would be no further play, when they said we were going back on at 5.10 pm. Our view was that the light was no better and had it been twice as good we would have struggled against the quicker bowlers.

I was soon out, beaten by a delivery from Hogg which I barely saw and caught low at third slip; by now Randall was getting really angry. The Aussies upset him by appealing for a catch at slip which did not carry, he swept Yardley angrily for four and then appealed against the light again. No joy. So he belted Yardley for six, glowered, tugged at his cap and generally looked most un-Randall. The umpires conceded at 5.45 that the light was too poor to continue; England 60–2 and a pretty eventful day ...

Second day

When Derek Randall takes ninety minutes to score 19 runs you know you are in a Test match. Devotees of World Series Cricket might not understand it, Kerry Packer might not fancy paying for it, but real Test matches are all about pressure and determination, the will to fight back and the character to battle through. Randall's struggle on the second morning was more than a surprising statistic; it was a sure sign that Australia were fighting for their lives.

When Australia might have broken through they dropped Randall at first slip – and that is the kind of mistake which can be punished so heavily in Test cricket. Yallop was the non-catcher and frankly, as slip catches go, it was perfectly straightforward; we chorused, 'That's out!' as soon as it left the bat but Yallop palmed it, let it slip, juggled again, had another grab and finally finished up flat on his back. Cosier replaced him at first slip not long afterwards; I wondered if the Aussies had a rule whereby anyone who drops a catch goes to the bottom of the class!

Randall caused one moment of merriment when he chased down to the sightscreen to move a sign which was troubling Bob Taylor, but there was precious little lightheartedness for the rest of the morning. The pressure was on, runs were dreadfully difficult to come by, and even Randall could not extract a giggle out of that situation.

It was all the more frustrating for him because he was in good form and fancied himself to get on with it. But the early bowling was aggressive, Laughlin and Cosier came on bowling to widespread fields; the innings practically ground to a halt. It was hardly Randall's cup of tea and the pressure began to get through to him; he became edgy and annoyed, aware of the taunts from the crowd and a slow handclap which broke out from time to time. Finally he took an impetuous slash at a wide delivery from Hurst and was brilliantly caught, one-handed, by Laughlin at gully.

Yallop immediately brought back Hogg, who has a habit of flinging himself off his feet in his exuberance, and came at us hard. Brearley tried to get inside the line of a delivery which lifted into his body and was caught down the leg-side off his glove; two deliveries later Taylor played back and was lbw. His stint as nightwatchman had lasted for nearly three hours.

England 120–5 and Australia suddenly sensed that they might force themselves back into the match. Gower and Botham had to re-establish the innings. A wicket or two would have exposed the England tail. Yallop quite rightly kept both his strike bowlers flat out in an attempt to break through. The atmosphere became electric.

It was an extraordinary situation. Australia racing in, lifted by the crowd whose mood had changed from frustration to aggression, faced by two batsmen whose only idea of defence was to attack. Both slogged and cleaved, played and missed; the crowd became incensed and the bowlers ran in faster and faster, sure that they must get a wicket with the next ball or the one after that ...

Botham was bounced by Hurst, hooked Hogg for two, slashed Hurst over slip; Gower played and missed, hooked forcefully – every risky shot in the game was being played twice an over and Australia felt they must break through. Yet the partnership put on 50 in fifty-seven minutes; the fast bowlers needed a rest.

Tactically, Yallop was in something of a quandary because his second-line attack was nowhere near as formidable as Hurst and Hogg in harness. But they had to be spelled and both were withdrawn in the space of four minutes; Botham and Gower knew that the new ball was due around tea and determined to cash in for the next forty minutes or so. Against Laughlin and Yardley they had every chance.

It was still a rare mixture of class and slash. Gower played a superb cut off Yardley for four – the shot of a fine player – and then had a huge slash and missed the ball completely; Botham heaved Yardley over his head for two fours in succession, mis-timed a great hoick to deep mid-on and was dropped despite a valiant gallop and dive by Higgs.

At tea England were 176-5 and the balance was back in our favour. One supporter paraded a Union Jack in front of the scoreboard and was pelted with empty beer cans for his presumption. It was a good time to be flying the flag but not the best of places!

Australia took the new ball soon after tea, Hogg steamed in and Gower and Botham carried on regardless – Gower elegant through the covers for four and three, Botham four through the slips, 11 off the first new-ball over!

Inevitably, Botham's sheer aggressiveness was his downfall. He took a huge heave at a delivery from Hogg – the ball would probably have landed somewhere in the Woolloongabba river – and was caught behind. He evidently thought that the ball had brushed his thigh and not his bat.

Gower square drove Hurst beautifully for four but drove without using his feet at the next ball and was caught behind. And that highlighted his lack of experience.

Yallop had fallen into the trap of over-bowling his fastest pair. They were flagging, obviously in need of a rest, and Gower should have spotted the fact. He should have played out a couple of overs once Botham had gone and given himself another chance against the second-line bowlers. As it was, Hogg had Edmonds magnificently caught by Maclean – a truly startling catch at full stretch down the leg-side – but there was nobody with enough pace and energy left to confront Old when he came in. Yallop had to call up Higgs and Old is rather partial to slow bowling.

Obviously, Yallop could only use the resources given to him and understandably he wanted to bowl his fastest men as long as possible in the hope of striking us out. But there comes a time when a captain has to cut his losses and give his strike bowlers a rest, however dangerous they seem to be, if the score is being pushed along. I felt he would have been better resting one of his fast men earlier instead of getting into a stop-go situation. Old and Miller put on 31 before poor light ended play five minutes early with England 257-8.

Third day

We have a theory in Yorkshire that if Chris Old middles the ball during the first couple of overs he will be out cheaply; if he plays and misses a few times he is in good nick. It sounds bizarre, I know, but it is often proved to be the key to his performances as a batsman. Old played and missed a few times against Hurst and Hogg; it was a good omen.

Mike Brearley told both batsmen to play their normal game but I suggested to Chris that it was vitally important they stay there for an hour. The day was already hot in contrast to the overcast conditions of the first two days, Willis's sore feet were a great worry to us all and it would be an enormous advantage if we could leave ourselves a five-hour rather than six-hour day in the field. On top of that, every run England scored now was worth double because we were in front.

Miller was out in Hogg's second over to a delivery which

nipped back a bit and trapped him lbw, but Old was beginning to strike the ball confidently and although Willis did not look comfortable he did not get out either. The fact that Old plays and misses early on often works to his advantage because bowlers put in an extra slip or gully and leave gaps in the outfield; when he does middle the ball he has plenty of choice.

Yallop brought on his legspinner, Higgs, which was tempting providence with Old at the wicket, and the batsmen had a brief conference. I thought Old would have had a go at Higgs but instead he played him very cautiously, perhaps conscious of the need to stay there for the first hour at least. It was against Old's natural inclinations but it was good policy.

A pause for drinks indicated that the first hour was up and we were still batting, but soon afterwards Willis played a splendid square drive for four and was out, caught behind, next ball. The last wicket had put on 20 precious runs and England had made 286, a lead of 170.

Australia's second innings began even more sensationally than their first. The breeze had freshened and changed so Bob Willis opened up from the pavilion end – and his first delivery swung in, seamed and took Cosier's off stump. It was a great moment for England but even so I felt for Cosier. He was batting out of position, run out for one in the first innings and now out first ball, and all that in front of his home crowd. Cosier had just signed a contract worth $500,000 to him over ten years and I could hear the derisive comments as he walked back to the pavilion. He must have felt as though his world had caved in. I know how he felt.

Mike Brearley opened with Ian Botham from the far end, partly because Old was a bit breathless after his batting stint and partly because the wind would help Botham's swing. England are lucky in that their first-choice change bowler also likes to get his hands on the new ball; Botham uses the new ball a lot for Somerset and he doesn't need asking twice. He was bowling against the wind but that is far less of a disadvantage for Botham than most because he is so strong. That full body pivot at delivery means he can generate real pace even with a gale blowing into his face.

Toohey didn't last long. He played and missed at Botham's

second delivery and was then beaten by a straightish inswinger which caught him half forward and trapped him lbw. Australia were 2–2 and desperately needed to dig in; Wood seemed to be on edge and had one or two hair-raising misunderstandings which left Yallop stretching to regain his ground, but they hung on to lunch.

We were still in a very strong position and Willis and Old really stripped themselves to try and force a breakthrough after lunch. Considering that his feet were giving him considerable pain, Willis bowled a superb line; we thought he had Yallop caught behind for 19 – off his glove hooking – but umpire French thought otherwise. Poor Willis doubled up in disbelief. It was hot and humid, the batsmen were playing defiantly and Willis and Old were beginning to blow a bit, but just when it looked as though we might be frustrated for a long spell Old broke through. Wood was playing well over to protect his off stump, as in the first innings, when Old pitched one middle-and-off and hurried it into him; he was cramped for room and practically falling over when the ball hit his pads.

Yallop had begun to play his shots qute confidently, especially off the back foot, and we had to put a mid-off in for the first time. So when Geoff Miller replaced Old, Brearley asked him to concentrate on keeping the runs down.

Miller, bowling fairly flat into the wind, did a very good job under orders. He got one to bounce and turn appreciably; it probably hit the edge of the rough, and that obviously preyed on Yallop's mind. And Hughes, trying to pull, lobbed the ball off the toe of the bat between me at midwicket and Botham just in front of square. So neither batsman felt like taking any liberties with him and even Yallop, a very good player of spin, was reduced to stealing singles to cover.

The partnership put on 50 in ninety minutes and was clearly becoming a bit of a nuisance. The pitch had flattened out considerably, in fact the only real problem was the odd delivery which hit the cracks and kept low; our bowlers were working hard without finding a way through and even Botham could not reproduce his usual knack of breaking partnerships. But he had a fascinating duel with Hughes in the attempt.

Hughes played forward far too often for Botham's self-respect and it became obvious that sooner or later he would get a bouncer. At least, it was obvious to me because I was fielding in the danger area at fine leg, with plenty of time to reflect that I was in the firing line – and downwind ...

Botham bounced, Hughes hooked and the ball whistled in my direction like a shell. I was still ten or twelve yards away when it smashed into the fence without bouncing; had I got in the way it would have taken me with it. Brearley put me right back and moved Gower three-quarters deep behind square; Botham tempted him and Hughes promptly smashed the ball into the boundary picket. So Gower went right back on to the boundary, Hughes ducked and picked his moment and then pulled Botham powerfully for four through midwicket. There was a lot going on between batsman and bowler but Australia were having the better of it. They had been under real pressure at lunch; by tea they were 102–3, on target to equalling our score before the end of the day.

Mike Brearley made it clear he expected a special effort in the last session; we had been in the field for only three hours and the next day was rest day so it was not unreasonable to expect a bit extra. The ball was thirty-one overs old, two batsmen were well established and unless we framed ourselves we might lose what advantage we had. But Bob Willis's feet were still a major worry. He took his boots off and bathed them during tea; our physiotherapist Bernard Thomas worked on him like a second in a boxer's corner between rounds. We needed a breakthrough.

Miller again bowled tightly and very effectively. Gower was alive to it when Hughes tried to push on the off-side for singles, so Hughes had to risk sweeping to keep himself ticking over; Yallop's chief scoring shot off Miller became a push to mid-on and a breathless race for a single.

Willis simply could not bowl flat out on dreadfully sore feet so he cut down his pace, concentrated on bowling a good line and even cut out his bouncer after Hughes had hooked one fifteen yards over the fence. Botham in turn cut out the bouncer – the ball was too old, the pitch too good and the batsmen too entrenched. A significant victory for Hughes.

Hughes had done particularly well, not just because he made

51 not out when poor light stopped play but because he had shown real character and determination in a very difficult situation. His temperament was supposed to be suspect but there was precious little sign of that today. Yallop was 74 not out, Australia were only thirteen behind on 157-3 ... an afternoon's work they could be proud of.

I managed to get one spectator into trouble. He was daft enough or drunk enough to parade in front of the scoreboard hill bar with a T shirt which read: Boycott King Pom, and the Aussies there weren't having that. They showered him with empty beer cans, ripped the shirt from his back and burned it. Honestly, I never said a word.

Fourth day

Graham Yallop was reported in some morning papers as saying Australia could still win the Test. Encouraging the troops is all very well and he could hardly announce be expected to lose, but in the circumstances I felt he was being unduly optimistic. To win, Australia needed to bat another day and perhaps an hour on the last morning. Then they would have five hours in which to bowl England out for less than about 240. All we needed was a breakthrough.

It was ninety-five minutes before we made it, by which time Hughes and Yallop had added 62 runs and left the previous Australian fourth wicket record at Brisbane well behind. They looked confident against the early attack of Botham, Miller and Edmonds, confident when Willis took the new ball – and it was confidence which finally became Yallop's undoing.

Yallop was on the back foot driving on the up, the shot of a confident, perhaps over-confident, man against the new ball, when Willis flung out his right hand on his follow-through and made a brilliant reflex catch. Yallop threw back his head as though he could not believe his eyes, Willis hurled the ball twice the height of the pavilion in triumph.

A great innings from Yallop in the circumstances, but for all his heroics Australia were still deep in trouble. Laughlin was out cheaply, lbw to a delivery from Old which nearly took his toecap off, and Australia were still only 58 in front with five wickets down. We knew they would make a fight of it – and in fact they braved it out until just after 5.00 pm – but we also knew the Test was in our grasp.

We might just have finished them off quicker but Willis was hobbling. He was obviously in a lot of pain though he rarely mentioned it and never complained. I suggested that when he finished his bowling spell he should change into plimsolls for fielding, and his first reaction was that he would be forever falling on his bottom – or words to that effect. But he gave it a try, and if he wasn't exactly greased lightning round the boundary we could forgive him for that.

Maclean likes to cut so Miller gave him absolutely no room. In Australia's plight Maclean dared not slog but he likes to attack the spinners and the enforced discipline obviously did not suit him. We had one confident shout for lbw against him when he swept at Miller, but Australian umpires seldom give anything on the front foot. I reckoned it would have been given nine times out of ten in England.

The next ball had him in a hopeless tangle. He half made up his mind to sweep, tried to adjust as Miller drifted the ball away from him expertly and finished up trying to fend it away as it hit him on the back leg, clearly lbw. Yardley battled grimly for well over an hour under pressure from Miller until he got a fine edge to a straight-on ball and was caught low and left-handed by Brearley at slip. From extra cover I couldn't be sure whether the ball had carried and Yardley obviously thought it hadn't; he certainly showed no inclination to go until the square-leg umpire confirmed the decision.

Hogg is not the worst tail-end batsman in the world, a clean hitter if the ball is pitched up and a fine cutter of anything wide of the off stump. He got a couple round his ribs from Willis and shouted indignantly: 'How many's that?' to an umpire who obviously misunderstood the question. 'One to come', intoned the umpire, while England's slips fell about laughing.

Hogg made the mistake of angering Botham by pulling him through midwicket. A couple of bouncers, then a wickedly pacey delivery, well pitched up, saw him off. Hurst was bowled by a fast full toss two deliveries later and finally Edmonds plucked a fine catch out of the air with deceptive ease when

Hughes tried to farm the bowling by chipping Willis over midwicket.

England needed 170 to win and our first priority in the 45 minutes remaining that night was survival. Hogg found difficulty keeping his feet and went very wide of the crease, Yardley turned a couple in one over but our chief worry was the pressure put on the umpires by interminable appeals for lbw. Unfortunately, there are far too many appeals in Test cricket today compared with the earlier years of my Test career; in my view the situation is to be deprecated.

Fifth day

With 154 needed to win and a whole day to get them in there was no need to hurry – which makes it all the more ironic that anybody should be run out. I suppose that the fact that it was me and that Derek Randall was at the other end added some sort of spice for the reporters. Before that we lost Gooch, who was deceived by the angle when Hogg went wide and pushed a catch to slip.

I knew I was struggling as soon as Randall pushed the ball towards Toohey at extra cover and set off. He was on his way before he called and at Randall's pace a couple of seconds covers quite a lot of ground. I just put my head down and raced for the line; I didn't look at the fielder – I didn't have time – and I knew I was well out as soon as the throw hit.

I suppose some people would expect me to be angry, but I have run people out before and regretted it as soon as it happened. It is one of those foolish, unnecessary things; nobody wants it to happen but it happens all the same. I said, 'Good luck, keep going', as I passed Randall and he shouted: 'Don't worry, Fiery; I'm going to win it.' He did, too.

Brearley was caught behind cutting a delivery which was low and probably too close to the off stump to cut, but Randall and Gower rarely looked in much trouble. I did not understand Australia's field placings towards the end, when their only hope of winning the match was to grab a couple of wickets and try to put our tail under pressure.

Higgs bowled with Cosier at slip but nobody in a close catching position; there were a couple of bat-pads which didn't matter because the nearest fielder in front of the bat was twenty yards away. And when men were brought in – far too late – the field was split between close fielders and men out in the deep, the sort of positions normally used to combat tail-enders who will either prod or slog. Randall and Gower can both place the ball: I felt the whole fielding pattern was illogical.

It was fitting that Derek Randall should win the Man of the Match award, his second in successive Test matches in Australia. A year is a long time in a sportsman's life and Derek had experienced a great deal of disappointment in the months between the Centenary Test and the first Test at Brisbane. He came through it smiling and I suspect he always will.

7   In the heat of the moment

Sunday December 10th 1978 will no doubt find a cherished place in Geoff Boycott's life history, a red letter day for those who enjoy sensation and controversy far more than I do. I called an umpire an unrepeatable cheat: it was a stupid, mindless thing done in the heat of the moment and I regretted it soon afterwards. But it was said.

I will never really know how or why it happened, but perhaps events 12,000 miles away had something to do with it. I learned the night before that Yorkshire's Reform Group had failed in their attempt to censure the Yorkshire committee; I had been married to the county for seventeen years, a love match as far as I was concerned, and now the divorce papers had been served. It was the culmination of months of pressure and even I can only take so much.

The Press wanted my reaction to the Yorkshire decision and when I refused to comment – how could I say anything meaningful with the decision only a few hours old? – they did what the Press usually do. They became cutting and critical, as if it was my job to fill their columns for them. They smile and then they stab – and they think the next time they come along for a comment you are going to forget the wounding things they write and obligingly talk to them. Photographers want a picture and expect you to pose: if not they snatch a picture when they can. I know that is the media's job – heaven knows they parrot the phrase often enough – but they do not have to be so cynical and so pretentious.

I was full up, fed up, emotionally exhausted. I had spent two months on tour trying to appear calm with everything churning me up inside. Then Hughes got his pad in front of a delivery from Botham which I thought would have hit his middle stump about kneecap high – and the umpire turned down the appeal. Something snapped and the words tumbled out. There was no excuse but perhaps there was a reason.

I had never met the umpire, Don Weser, before. It was suggested in some quarters that I had an axe to grind because two umpiring decisions had gone against me in the match, but neither of them involved Weser. My remarks weren't made out of pique or malice, just on the spur of the moment.

'What did you say?' the umpire asked, and I repeated what I'd said. It all happened so quickly I never stopped to think. I don't suppose I am the first man in the world that has happened to.

Mike Brearley tapped me on the shoulder during a break for drinks. 'You shouldn't have said that. I don't think you're in the best position to judge lbw at mid-off and in any case you should apologise for calling him a cheat,' he said. I was still upset and as a Yorkshireman I don't back down too easily. 'I still think it was out and I'm a pretty good judge after all these years,' I said. We left it at that.

Doug Insole saw me at the end of the day. 'Did you call the umpire a cheat?' he asked.

I told him I had and that I had already decided to apologise. Doug told me I should not have said what I did and suggested it would be a good thing if I apologised as soon as possible.

We were not sure where the umpires' room was so Doug asked the Local Secretary how to get there and I went to see the umpire. The Press suggested later that Insole had to instruct me to go – and remember all this was happening before they got wind that anything was wrong – but that is utter rubbish. He did not have to force me to apologise.

I apologised to Weser in the umpires' room and he said that nobody had ever called him a cheat before but that we all made mistakes. He said he was going to report me but since I had come to apologise he wouldn't do so. The other umpire Don Hawks reminded me that I had been asked again on the field and that I did repeat it; and that I was an experienced player who ought to think before speaking.

I told them that I had had time to think and I apologised for what I had said and I referred to personal pressures and decisions against me in the match which hadn't helped.

We went on to discuss lbw and bat-pad decisions which Hawks had given against me and Don Hawks said that he had had no doubts about them. I didn't pursue our discussion or indicate that I thought the ball would have missed leg stump in the first innings.

I had gone to apologise to one umpire, shaken hands with him, and ended up discussing the pros and cons of two decisions with his partner.

In the professional game there is nothing unusual about batsmen discussing decisions with the umpires after the event. It's purely a technical thing with the batsmen wanting to know exactly what the ball did and where it pitched.

Doug was waiting for me when I left the umpires' room but I was still too upset to talk at length. I had told him earlier in the day that I wanted to have a talk about something which had been troubling me for some time. But the events of the day had overtaken that; everything was buzzing round my head.

I told the manager I did not want to play in the second Test. The way things were, I was not in the right frame of mind. I had had enough and there were players who could do a far better job for the team than I could. Quitter Boycott? No – honest enough to feel that we were on tour to win Test matches and that I was not likely to help England do that in my state of mind. Doug asked me if I wanted to talk about it but I was too upset. I practically broke down on the balcony in front of the dressing rooms and slipped away to my car to compose myself. Clive Radley and Graham Gooch came over to see if I was OK and Bernie Thomas suggested I went to his room later for a chat; I calmed down a bit and went back to the hotel.

We finished the match early next morning and Mike, Doug and I met to talk over the situation and especially my frame of mind with the Test match only a couple of days away. They were both very considerate – and insistent that I should play.

Mike pointed out that I had played well defensively at Brisbane. 'I know you are struggling to get the ball away but you still played as well as most. And we need somebody like you who can stay there and see off the new ball.'

Doug agreed. He told me that I had the temperament and the ability and that in terms of my record alone I was virtually an automatic choice for the whole series, and that to leave me out would only create problems. He said that everyone knew that I was under a lot of strain and would do everything to help.

The Yorkshire business wouldn't go away and would be with me for some time to come and I must not let it get on top of me. My best answer was to play and get runs to get my mind off everything else. All I needed was a long innings.

It was a confidence-boosting job, I know that. But I also feel that Doug was sincere and I felt that his approach said he knew something of my reactions and feelings. I appreciated that a lot.

The Press got hold of the story, writing along the lines that I had been reported for my remarks to the umpire. That was true in a sense but I was only part of the report, not the subject of it. Weser said he had included in his report the fact that an incident had occurred involving me and that it had been amicably settled, but the Press reports that I had 'been reported' overlooked all that. It was the truth but not the whole truth.

Naturally, the Press were insistent. They wanted to talk to me but I had nothing to tell them: Doug said the matter had been discussed – a lot more fully and openly than they realised – and had been settled. About the same time there was a story that I intended to quit the tour and go home; it didn't take some Pressmen long to suggest that I might in fact be sent home! I never considered going home – I might have said at some time or other that I would like to be home for Christmas but who the hell wouldn't – and I wasn't aware of any move to pack me off. But the papers enjoyed themselves.

There was one thing troubling me a lot which I discussed with the manager: it was that Mike Brearley seemed somewhat reluctant to consult me. The match against Western Australia, which we won by 140 runs in little over two days, was an extraordinary game, not least because we opted to bat after winning the toss. It was a decision with which I cannot agree; if we had put them in we would have won by an innings and the fact that we won convincingly at the end was due entirely to the ability of our bowlers.

But I was not consulted, even though Bob Willis was not playing in the game. He did ask Botham if he thought it would swing, but what that has to do with the appreciation of pitches and Australian conditions I really do not know. I have played in seventy-five Test matches and toured Australia more often than anyone in the party; I considered I had something to offer by way of advice and experience. I felt left out and I was angry because some people were ready to suggest I was actually unwilling to contribute to the team effort. Henry Blofeld suggested as much in a Sunday newspaper article but then, as now, Blofeld is frequently long on opinions and short on facts.

My main complaint about certain Pressmen through the years is that they will express opinions unsupported by the facts which are so easy for them to check – opinions which I think are irresponsible and often capable of causing great difficulties for the player in the public eye. No one minds fair comment based on truth; every player is entitled to complain of unfair and often mischievous comment based on inaccurate facts. In journalistic terms I believe it is called 'flying a kite'.

I had blown my top about not being consulted when I went to watch a replay of my lbw dismissal on TV and that was reported – via Chris Martin-Jenkins of the BBC and Peter Loader, I believe – to Mike Brearley and the manager. If I didn't want to be involved I would hardly have been playing hell about it.

The upshot was that I discussed it with Doug Insole and a couple of days later, at the team's pre-Test dinner, Mike said quietly: 'I understand you are upset about not being asked for advice.' I think it helped to clear the air and, as I mention later, things worked out very well.

The match itself was an incredible affair. The pitches at Perth used to be hard, fast, bouncy and true, but this one had a cushion of grass on it and was damp underneath. Even when the sun shone the ball seamed and moved about alarmingly.

We were bowled out for 144 and would have got nowhere near that but for a fine performance from Tolchard and some spirited batting from Edmonds and Emburey later on. Then we bowled out Western Australia for 52 – their lowest ever total in twenty-eight matches against the English touring team – and I doubt they would have got that many if Hendrick had been brought on earlier. The pitch was tailormade for him but he did not get the new ball. When he finally did he took 5–11.

Batting was still the devil's own job when we went in again and this time we were bowled out for 126. But that still meant Western Australia had to score 219 to win and nobody fancied their chances in the circumstances. Botham and Hendrick got among them and they fell apart, all out for 78 after thirty-three minutes of the third day. It was the first defeat suffered by Western Australia in three years but then I don't suppose they play on a pitch like that every five minutes.

The early finish gave us a little unexpected time off but I used it for practice. What with one thing and another, I felt I needed it.

8   A professional victory

Second Test – *first day*

I felt at the time that the first day at Perth could be the most important in the 1978–9 series from England's point of view. Australia had us in desperate trouble on three for two and then 41–3; they were poised to bounce back and perhaps square the series after losing in Brisbane. And then their confidence would have been sky-high; it might have been an enormous psychological blow in their favour. Instead we batted back into the game and finished the day 190–3; we felt their confidence ebb and their enthusiasm wane a little. Important hours.

We had some difficulty in naming our side. Old had a back strain, Miller was doubtful because of a stomach upset and Willis's feet were still sore and painful. He had visited several specialists and received all kinds of advice on how to cure the trouble; it was even suggested that the long-term cure was amputation of one of the toes of his left foot! But Willis said he felt a lot happier, Miller declared himself fit after a day in bed and Old's injury enabled the selectors to make a place for Mike Hendrick, which they would have done in any case.

There was still the problem of whether to play Edmonds or John Lever – and what to do if we won the toss. And since my talk to the manager I was glad to find I was among those asked my opinion on both counts.

I said I would put them in. The pitch had been saturated since the West Australia match, not just sprinkled but flooded, and the water had been rolled into the strip. Whatever it looked like on the surface there was obviously a lot of moisture underneath. The outfield had been well sprinkled, too, so it would be lush and green; runs would be very difficult to come by.

Edmonds or Lever? I reckoned that the pitch had been

watered to bind it together. There were veins of grass but quite a few cracks too – and if the sun was hot for the first three or four days the cracks would open and we might be glad of Edmonds in the side.

The selectors decided against Edmonds, partly because they were understandably anxious to have some insurance in case Willis broke down. And it seemed to me at that time that Mike might have lost a bit of confidence in Phil Edmonds' bowling and might not have been happy at putting him on to bowl.

Mike decided he would not show his hand a minute before he had to. If Australia knew in advance that we were playing four seamers they would obviously conclude we intended putting them in, so there was no doubt what they would do to us if they won the toss. He handed over the team sheet as he and Yallop were walking out for the toss, and as it turned out Yallop was already thinking along similar lines.

It was desperately hard work. Australia opened with Hogg and the left-arm seamer Dymock, perhaps because they felt I was vulnerable to Hogg and unhappy against left-arm bowlers, which is not a new theory. The ball swung a little in the wind and cut off the pitch alarmingly; we needed a secure start and instead we lost two wickets in no time.

Gooch tried to drive on the up – I fancy he does that a bit more than he should for an opening batsman not in the best of form – and was caught behind, then Randall was out for a duck. He received a superb bouncer from Hogg, the quickest delivery of the day rearing from just short of a length, and touched his cap in mock nonchalance after it had almost taken his head off. Then he played a very indecisive shot. The delivery was short and he might have played it defensively on the back foot but he shaped to play a half pull, half hook, intending to help the ball on its way rather than hit it violently, and then changed his mind. He virtually let the ball hit the bat and it lobbed to Wood just behind square leg.

The ball seamed about, shot through when it pitched on a grassy area and lifted alarmingly from just short of a length; it was impossible to get on the front foot and hard to imagine where the next run was coming from. We scored ten in the first hour and Hogg bowled 6.7 overs before conceding a run !

The pressure was intense and the Aussies increased it by appealing for everything that hit the pad. It's an old trick, part enthusiasm and part gamesmanship, designed to keep the batsmen on edge and put a little extra pressure on the umpires. Yallop and Cosier were shouting at the bowlers from the slips, urging them on, the atmosphere was electric and Brearley and I had the devil's own job just to survive.

We made it, gratefully, to lunch and the lads in the dressing room were delighted with the way we had stuck it out. 'If you had got out early we could have been five or six down now,' Brearley told me. And that was encouraging because I was worried at my inability to score quicker. 'If I go on like this I won't get fifty in the day' – but the lads were happy enough for me to stay there.

I was particularly puzzled by the offspinner Yardley. Normally I am a pretty confident player of offspin but I can't work him out at all; there is something distinctly strange about his action. He keeps beating me for length and after lunch I was in a real state – forward when I should have been back and *vice versa*. I felt as though I was doing a quickstep.

Brearley lifted the second ball of the twenty-seventh over for our first boundary soon after lunch, but then he tried to steer a widish delivery from just short of a length square on the off-side and nicked it to the wicketkeeper. At 41–3 we were still in trouble; a couple more quick wickets and it was quite possible we could be bowled out for less than 100. And Australia were well aware of that.

Gower was in a bit of trouble at first, uncertain whether to hook, duck or block the ball chest-high. He ducked into one from Hogg, turned his head away and was hit on the neck behind the ear-shield, but surprisingly he indicated it hadn't hurt much.

Gower played magnificently. He is quite the best timer of a ball I have seen and the fact that he plays and misses a little too often for his own good does not alter that judgement. He is a lucky cricketer and nobody should begrudge him that, even if Hogg called him a distinctly uncomplimentary name after being hit for four and was reprimanded by umpire Tom Brooks.

Brooks is very good in situations like that. He looks rather austere and aloof from the ringside but he is a knowing, calm person on the field – a stickler for the laws and a firm disciplinarian but not the sort of man to make a scene. Hogg was told firmly to mind his manners; no more needed to be said.

I could not muster many runs myself in the hour before tea but I encouraged Gower to talk between overs and to concentrate when he was at the non-striker's end. The only friend you have in the middle is the guy at the other end; I did not want to dissuade Gower from playing his sort of game but I did want to make him think hard about things. He was going well; I was still holding the fort.

The worst trouble I got into was against Hurst. I knew I was not playing forward enough, partly through lack of confidence and form, and I was trying to get forward when he let me have a short one. I was half way through a hook when I realised it would be on me too quickly and I got in a complete mess; I just fell out of the way and hoped it wouldn't connect. It didn't but the Aussies went up for a catch behind and made a real song and dance about it. They appealed any number of times when deliveries which hit the pad were obviously doing too much, and the fact that batsmen clearly nicked the ball into their pads didn't prevent them going up either. I thought we would all be deaf by the end of the day.

Every player is proud of his first century in Ashes cricket but Gower has reason to remember his with special pride. Considering the state of the game and the nature of the attack he faced, it was a marvellous century, a personal triumph for him and a real boost for England when we dearly needed one. Characteristically, he did not hang about; it took him 214 minutes, which was very quick in the circumstances.

I was 63 not out at the end of the day, pleased to have done a job but still acutely aware that I could play a lot better. I was determined not to give it away and several things helped in that – encouragement from the players, a couple of Union Jacks round the ground, the Pom who ran up as I walked off at tea and said: 'Don't give up; they're frightened of you.' I felt my concentration was sharpening after a spell without a long innings.

The lads were delighted with our position. Any side which is put in to bat and then makes 190–3 on the first day is entitled to feel satisfied. Doug Insole said I had made 'A very valuable contribution'. I felt so too.

Second day

If I needed confirmation of that, the abusive telegrams didn't take long to arrive. Jack Birney, a member of the House of Representatives and one of Australia's more publicity-conscious politicians, dropped me a little note: 'You have done for Australian cricket what the Boston Strangler did for door-to-door salesmen', which was a compliment, if not a very original one. Just in case the media mis-spelled his name, he sent a copy to the Press box. I did not see any newspaper which used it.

The Cricket Lovers of Australia had a whip round and came up with: 'Congratulations on your laborious 19 before lunch. Memories of Bradman.'

And a gentleman from Perth cabled: 'Not since Trevor Bailey in Brisbane in 1958 has such a deplorable performance been staged in a Test match. Your ability to avoid great fast bowlers is legendary. You have done much to destroy a century of great Test cricket today. You lack all ability expected in an opening batsman, you lack all the necessary ingredients that make for a great opening batsman and you are the antithesis of J. B. Hobbs. You have converted one million Australian Packer fans.' England really must have had a good day.

When I fielded on the fence later in the day the local loud-mouths held their usual competition in witless, foul-mouthed remarks. Some remarks from the crowd can be amusing, even in Australia where I don't exactly expect them to be on my side, but these were just obscene and mindlessly crude. The favourite taunt, of course, was Packer – which shows how much that section of the crowd know about real Test cricket.

They can take their beer even less than they can take real cricket, a disgrace to themselves and an affront to the majority of Australian spectators who appreciate and enjoy the tussle, the shades and meanings of the game. When you hear the yobs you realise that their very loud mouthed utterances give the Australians generally a reputation of being bad losers, and unfortunately their stupidity rubs off on some of the youngsters who go to the Tests and who think it's clever to be rude and foul-mouthed. I hope the trend doesn't continue.

Mike Brearley said the first forty minutes of the morning could be vital; it was important we did not lose a wicket. But Hogg went round the wicket to Gower and beat him with one which pitched on the off stump and hit the off stump – a fine delivery considering the angle and the pace at which Hogg bowls. David looked crestfallen but he had done a marvellous job; he had played quite magnificently and I told him so as he went past.

Botham and I reckoned that Hogg would bowl in short bursts and determined to see him off. He bowled round the wicket to me, firing the ball into my ribs and trying for a catch at leg slip or short square leg. Yallop spoke to him during drinks and I got the impression he told him to sacrifice a bit of pace for accuracy because some of his deliveries were fearfully wild. The next two deliveries were well below top pace and I played them carefully. 'For Chrissake, Fiery, have a go at them,' moaned Hogg – and when the next delivery jumped and hit me on the glove his language was unprintable. Exasperation was getting home.

Hurst seemed to be coming in a bit quicker today. He is a difficult customer because at the instant before delivery he is looking at fine leg and it's always difficult to judge the length of the ball. Botham should have been forward because we knew Hurst skims the ball through, but he was playing from the crease and trapped lbw by one which came back. I should have been forward too but I played back, deceived by the length again, and was caught plumb. Two wickets in ten deliveries from Hurst, England 224–6, and Australia must have fancied they had finally broken through.

But Miller played exceptionally well, a fine innings and I don't base that assessment solely on his statistical contribution of 40 runs. He looked very composed, well balanced and moved his feet admirably, even though he had not had many runs on tour so far. Innings of 12 from Taylor and 14 from Lever may not look much in the scorebook but at that stage of the game they were very valuable – and runs still weren't easy to make.

Even after they got out there was a bizarre little stand of 14 between Hendrick and Willis, the sort of partnership which drives bowlers who are already tired to distraction. Willis got off the mark with one of the finest shots of the tour, a studious drive through midwicket which was fielded at cover, but came to grief when he managed to hit the ball fifty yards straight up in the air. Yallop was waiting when it came out of orbit: England 309 all out.

It was a remarkable performance considering we had been put in and remembering the struggles of the first day, certainly far beyond anything we banked on getting. We would have been happy with 220. But Australia could be well pleased with the performance of Hogg, who finally scuppered the suggestion that he lacks the stamina to sustain a new-ball attack. Five wickets for 65 off thirty eight-ball overs hardly suggested he lacked ability or strength; and he will get better.

Brearley and Yallop got together before the start of their innings to clarify the position regarding bouncers to tail-end batsmen. We felt that Hogg was too competent a batsman to be protected by his position at number nine and said so; Botham was especially peeved that Hogg could bounce him but that he had to wait until Hogg was relatively established before he could retaliate. If we bounced Hogg, they would bounce our number nine, who happened to be John Lever. 'I'm sorry, JK,' said Brearley, 'but I've had to trade you for Hoggy.' General merriment. 'Oh charming: thanks very much,' says JK.

Brearley also said he did not expect any moaning or cussing if decisions went against us. 'They have had a hell of a lot of shouts for lbw turned down and perhaps we have been lucky with one or two. So let's not get carried away if we have decisions turned down as well,' he said.

We opened with Botham and Lever, partly because we felt Botham would swing it in a strong crosswind and partly because we fancied Lever against the left-hander Wood. Lever bowled Wood cheaply in the State match and we had a suspicion that Wood hadn't worked him out at all: the plan was to give him a couple of overs and then bring on Willis if he hadn't broken through.

Lever took only ten deliveries. He swung one into Wood

and although there was a suspicion that his leg might have been outside the line the umpire had no doubts. Another vitally important early breakthrough.

Hughes looked pretty self-assured – after his century in the first Test he was entitled to – and drove Botham confidently off the front foot. Willis bowled him several inswingers, including one that almost cut him in two, but then produced a delivery which pitched on the off stump and held up. The stump was broken at its base and the groundsman had to come on to ferret the spike out of the ground.

I was surprised when Brearley asked the umpire to take time off for the stoppage, important when we came to calculate the overs rate. 'They can do that; it's an act of God,' grinned Brearley. It's coming to a pretty pass when batsmen have acts of God to contend with ...

Australia had quite enough problems with acts of Willis. Twelve deliveries after dismissing Hughes he forced Yallop on to the back foot and beat him with a very full delivery, almost a half volley, which flicked the off stump. I think Yallop would have done better to go forward but that hadn't come easily to any batsman in the match. Willis galloped away in a wide semi-circle while we chased after him to offer our congratulations.

Darling and Toohey tried to dig in and Darling looked better than I had seen him. He drove nicely and tucked the ball nimbly off his feet for singles: but what he was thinking about in the last over of the day I will never know. There was absolutely no sense in looking for a single, least of all a quick one, when Toohey pushed the ball wide of Botham towards short midwicket. But Darling was already half way down the wicket, Botham pounced and beat him with his throw to Miller over the stumps and Darling was sensationally and senselessly run out. Australia 60–4.

Third day
The breeze was still fresh, blowing almost at right angles across the pitch, which at least spared some poor fast bowler the penance of running into it. They call the wind hereabouts the Freemantle Doctor; the temperature often climbs into the

nineties and beyond and it's the only thing that prevents the city from frying.

The captain's plan was to contain with Miller and Lever from one end and attack for wickets from the other. The odd delivery was turning and bouncing, largely because the grass acted like a spongy mat, so the spinners should be awkward.

Cosier didn't last long and never looked like settling down. After scores of one and nought in the first Test he was understandably edgy and was soon caught at fourth slip, driving Willis without using his feet. Miller put Maclean under pressure with four men round the bat and, sure enough, he swept far too early and lobbed a catch to silly point via his pad and the back of his bat. At 79–6 Australia were still fighting to avoid the follow-on.

Toohey gritted it out splendidly. He is an unusual player in that he always tries to get on to the front foot; he will play forward to practically everything and if the ball is short he drops his hands and sways the top half of his body out of the way. Like everybody else he had to fight for his runs, but he stuck at it when Australia needed somebody to shore up the innings.

Brearley brought on Lever in place of Willis, not a very good idea with Toohey and Yardley at the crease. Both are off-side players and would appreciate the ball slanting across them from the left-hander. Toohey played a magnificent cover drive and Randall made an equally magnificent stop; hard luck on Toohey because Randall had offered at the end of the previous over to swap places with me and stay at midwicket. When he skidded to pick up the ball he looked over and grinned; I would still have been galloping towards the boundary ...

As soon as Hendrick came on he had Yardley caught behind, but Hogg was as troublesome as ever. He was almost caught by Botham at short square leg off bat and pad and then survived only because Taylor fumbled momentarily after he was beaten by a quicker one down the leg side from Miller. It would have been a superb stumping, but that's the sort of standard we expect from Taylor these days. Hogg cut Hendrick for four and then slogged him past mid-on for three; Australia had avoided the follow-on and one pressure at least had eased.

Toohey began to get down the wicket to Miller and forced him for four through mid-on, looking much more confident once the follow-on had been saved.

Hogg probably still thinks he was cheated out soon after lunch but there was a definite click as the ball went through to Taylor. Hogg gestured angrily that the ball had brushed his thigh, but the fielders round the bat were convinced it was an inside edge – and so was Tom Brooks.

Dymock dug in, Toohey picked up ones and twos with growing fluency and we just could not break through. It was frustrating – and Ian Botham is a dangerous man in circumstances like those. He unleashed four bouncers in five deliveries against Toohey. The first two disappeared for four, the third sailed off the splice over my head at midwicket, and after the fourth ball had gone down the leg side the fifth was another bouncer banged for four. Good stuff to watch but not very thoughtful.

The situation cried out for a slower delivery or one pitched in the block hole. 'I intended to fool him with something different but half way through my run I thought, "I'll knock his head off"' said Botham later. And it doesn't make much sense to bowl four bouncers against an established batsman with a ball sixty-four overs old.

Bob Willis came stalking up from fine leg in a thunderous mood. 'Don't give that silly so and so the new ball,' he growled – and it was not difficult to understand his annoyance. Toohey had just scored fourteen runs in five deliveries and it had taken most batsmen an hour of very hard work to make as many as that; the new ball, a yard quicker and more dangerous, was only a few deliveries away.

Dymock had been in for well over an hour, so by the arrangement between the captains he was entitled to receive a bouncer. But Tom Brooks was not keen on the idea, especially with the new ball due. He and Brearley had quite a discussion about it and Mike insisted he could not instruct his fast bowlers not to let Dymock have a bouncer; Brooks said: 'That's up to you, but we will have to take whatever action we think fit.' As it turned out, Hendrick bowled Dymock in his first over with the new ball so it was all a bit academic, but the bouncer question is obviously one which is going to keep cropping up.

Umpires always come in for a bit of stick and I have felt myself badly done to before now; every batsman and every bowler in the game has. But one incident underlined just how difficult the job is and just how good a top-class umpire can be. Willis beat Hurst on the drive and everybody round the bat heard a nick; they all went up for a catch behind and Brooks wasn't exactly the most popular man on the ground when he turned it down. Then we noticed a tiny red bruise on the outside of the off stump – that's the nick we had heard and half a dozen very experienced cricketers would have sworn it was an inside edge. An impeccable piece of judgement by Brooks.

Australia were bowled out for 190, 119 behind, and we had two hours' batting to the close. Gooch and I made 58 and there was some suggestion in the Press that we should have gone quicker, but it is far better to be 58–0 than 75–3. A sound start is the basis for all big scores and Brearley knew this when he told us to play normally and avoid losing a wicket if possible; no targets were set.

Aussie were in a talkative mood. Cosier at bat-pad on the offside and Wood at short square leg exchanged a few pleasantries; 'Hoggy'll knock his head off in a minute', that sort of thing. And Hogg was pretty talkative himself. He very quickly decided he did not want Cosier in that position and told the captain so in no uncertain terms. 'I bowled thirty overs in the first innings; I should know where I want my ruddy fielders by now,' he protested. Yallop ran across and told him to get on with it.

I played forward to one from Dymock which pitched and left me and everybody went up for a catch behind. Not out – and the air was blue, caps were thrown to the ground, the Aussie players were cursing and swearing and half the crowd joined in. I did not believe I hit it so I did exactly what the Aussies do in those circumstances – I stayed where I was.

Not too long afterwards I ducked into a delivery from Hogg which didn't bounce. My head was just above the height of the bails when the ball hit the side of my skull and took off over the slips for four leg byes; it looked nasty but I confess I barely felt a thing. Hogg asked me later what kind of protection I wore under my cap; he just wouldn't believe that I didn't have some sort of metal skull-guard until I showed him my cap – and the lump.

We made it through to the close, which gave the innings a sound foundation. I was still not in very good form, playing too much on the leg-side and not getting forward enough. I needed to use my left hand more and I needed rhythm. Still, I played a couple of good shots off the back foot against Dymock which were not quite wide enough of the field, perhaps the rhythm was coming back slowly. So far I had scored my runs out of determination.

Fourth day

The intention was to get another 180 runs before tea. Brearley envisaged they may come at around 80 in the morning and 100 in the afternoon, but he also wanted us to play steadily for an hour and not to lose a wicket. A fair enough plan, but we never stayed on schedule.

The third ball of Hogg's second over nipped back a long way and hit the outside of my left pad as I shaped to play to leg. I thought it might have been missing but the umpire did not. Gooch had his luck – he was dropped by Hughes at slip off Hogg early in the day – but he deserved that after a difficult tour and he certainly took advantage with some fine shots: a square drive off Dymock, a cut off Hogg and a flip off the hip, all for four.

He had scored 43 when Hogg beat him with one which pitched just outside off stump, came back and hit him between both pads. Hogg thought it must have been out and danced himself into a frenzy when the appeal was turned down; Randall at the non-striker's end did a little jig just to show he's a better dancer. Two deliveries later Hogg had a much more hopeful shout and the appeal was upheld; I thought it had done too much.

Brearley was out first ball, caught in at least two minds by a delivery which started wide of the off stump and seamed into him. He seemed to decide to leave it, then played at it and gave a low catch to the wicketkeeper. England 93–3.

Randall looked in good form again, cutting and hooking

Dymock and pulling Hogg and Hurst down through mid-wicket: he might have made a really big score had he not done the umpire's job for him. When he was 45, Randall swept far too soon at Yardley and the ball looped off his wrist to Cosier at short leg. The impetus of his stroke carried Randall round and he strode off towards the pavilion without waiting for a verdict. And when he got there he announced he wasn't sure if he was out!

The ball had hit him fairly high – on the wrist; it was a very close decision whether it came off the cuff of the glove or fractionally higher. If he was not sure he should have let the umpire decide, and it would have been a fiendishly difficult decision. But that's what umpires are for.

Gower and Botham struggled a bit to lunch against Hurst and Yardley and we found ourselves in a peculiar situation. We had put on 92 for the loss of three wickets; 75-1 would have been much better. As it was, batsmen could not afford to attack wholeheartedly because a couple of wickets could have put us in trouble, and they could not defend because we wanted to win the match. A ticklish situation.

And it was soon even more awkward. Hogg went round the wicket to Gower and got one to bounce out of the footholds; it gloved him and stayed in the air for an unnerving long time. The next ball was short outside the off stump and I suspect Gower had the previous delivery on his mind; he tried to cut although it cramped him for room and was caught behind.

Bob Taylor had to have a runner because he was struggling a little with a groin strain, and there was a fair amount of dressing-room discussion as to who it should be. Taylor suggested Randall or Gooch – fairly bizarre alternatives – and somebody suggested me as the sprightliest – not to say the only – thirty-eight-year-old in the side. I was elected runner in a Test match once – for Colin Cowdrey at Edgbaston in 1968; he scored a century and I reckon I ran 90 of them! So I did the decent thing and nominated Mike Brearley. After all, what better opportunity for the captain to direct the tactics of his batsmen . . .

Derek Randall cut short the conversation. 'I'll do it; this is a serious game,' he said testily. When we had finished laughing,

Brearley asked him who would do the calling. 'Not me. I don't even call when I'm batting,' grinned Randall.

Botham and Miller had to work hard against Hogg but they gradually began to play their shots more confidently and it was obvious Hogg was very tired. Miller pulled and cut him, Botham drove lustily, Hogg looked heavy limbed.

Botham's enthusiasm got the better of him and he thumped a delivery from Yardley straight to Wood at deepish mid-off; not a very thoughtful shot considering he had hit two fours through mid-off and Wood had obviously been put there specifically to contain the stroke. Miller played some attractive strokes but we were dismissed for 203 – and disappointed with ourselves.

We had hoped to have thirty runs more and still have a few wickets in hand for a quick thrash after tea; instead we had been bowled out for 150 runs in the day. So much for the sages of the media who criticised Gooch and me for not throwing the bat at the ball on Sunday evening. Had we lost a couple of wickets then and been dismissed for fifty fewer runs, Australia would have had a target of less than 300 to win in a day plus a session – and that is not impossible. Some clown on the radio said when Brearley and I got out it was probably a good thing; the strokemakers can get on with it; I wonder what he said when we were all out at tea.

It has been proved time after time that the best way to ensure a big total in reasonable speed and safety is to build a solid foundation without losing wickets. That may take time, but it means that middle-order batsmen can go in and attack without worrying too much about losing wickets; they know exactly what their job is. Batsmen never do well when they are unsure of their priorities; I sensed that our middle order fell somewhere between two stools.

Australia needed 328 to win and on paper at least they were entitled to fancy their chances. 'I would sooner be in our position than theirs,' said Brearley, but there was a suspicion that we had made our job harder than it need be. I didn't give Australia a price of winning but a lot depended on how much faith they had in themselves.

Bad light stopped play not long after Australia opened their innings – but too late to save poor Rick Darling. He was hit in the box by a delivery from Willis and collapsed in the crease in terrible trouble; it must have been nearly ten minutes before he was able to continue. And in the next over Lever produced a murderous delivery.

There seemed to be a responsive patch on the pitch, perhaps the edge of a bowler's follow-through, and Lever hit it. The ball reared horribly, quite unplayable, and Darling had to fend it out of his face as best he could with both feet off the ground. The ball smacked the handle, plucked the bat out of Darling's hands and looped to me at mid-on.

Fifth day

Victory for either side was still a possibility and Australia should at least save it if they batted well, so the last day was intriguingly balanced. And Australia got off to a bright start in pursuit of 317 runs in the day.

That was partly because a shift in the wind upset our bowling rhythm. It changed round completely, so that Willis had to change ends in order to bowl downwind. He did not like that and the wind proved troublesome to Lever, taking the ball into Wood's pads and enabling him to punch it away through midwicket. Hughes square cut Willis magnificently for four and against an aggressive field, Aussie made a useful start.

Willis made the breakthrough with a delivery which lifted a little and crowded Hughes for room. He tried to force it rather than kill it and the ball slid off the face of the bat to Gooch at fourth slip. Australia 36–2.

Yallop was under a lot of pressure from the moment he came in. Five men in the slips, Miller complete with helmet at silly point; seven men all in catching positions close to the bat. He gloved one but it went down; he got a thick edge wide to Gooch's left hand at fourth slip and he played a firm defensive shot off the back foot through Miller's hands. Not a miss; it takes a brave man to stand at silly point for that sort of shot and it would have been an incredible catch. Yallop had braved it out for forty-three minutes for only three runs when he mistimed a leg glance and was caught behind after the ball brushed his pad.

Toohey – not out 81 in the first innings – went first ball this time and did not like the decision one bit. He pushed out to Hendrick without using his feet and was caught behind, though there was a suspicion he might have hit the ground and not connected with the ball. Suddenly 58–4, Australia were in serious trouble. And it might have been worse . . .

Botham cut down his pace, tried to swing the ball at medium pace and went round the wicket seeking the problem spot which had helped bring Darling's downfall. Wood skied a massive top edge in the general direction of midwicket.

I was at square leg and Lever was at widish mid-on; the ball was dropping into no-man's land and I ran backwards, looking into the sun, to get underneath it. The wind caught it as I tried to settle myself and drifted it away from me: it finally fell wide of my right shoulder as I dived and got a fingertip to it. Not the easiest catch I have ever tried to take but I am not making excuses. Wood was 28 and going well; it was a bad miss from the team's point of view and I was immediately conscious of the fact.

Eight runs later Wood did it again. This time the ball sailed high towards widish mid-on and Brearley shouted 'JK'; I hesitated and set off only when Lever himself called, 'Yours, Fiery!' I never got near it. Without the initital hesitation I might have made the distance but there was a foot or two of daylight between me and the ball when it came down. I don't call that a drop. The crowd did, of course, they loved it; and just to complete the fun I caught Wood soon afterwards – off a no ball!

Botham bowled well; Hendrick bowled magnificently, but Wood and Cosier battled past lunch and in fact put on 50 in only seventy-three minutes. Wood played far more sensibly after lunch – perhaps he had been reminded that Australia were saving the match – and Cosier was powerfully effective. Cosier is formidably strong. He often looks rather ungainly and he is certainly unorthodox: he played one slash for four over slips off Willis, which seemed like a wild shot except that I have seen him play it so many times before. The stand was worth 83 when Cosier swept extravagantly at Miller and was trapped lbw.

Australia collapsed completely. Maclean was deceived by Miller's change of pace after a cat-and-mouse spell; Hogg was drawn back and forward before Miller beat him with a quicker delivery – fine bowling in each case. But many of Australia's dying shots were deplorable; they lost their last six wickets for 20 runs and none of the late-order batsmen managed to hold us up for as long as half an hour.

Yardley fought for twenty-six minutes before he was superbly caught by Botham at second slip, but even his dismissal illustrated Australia's fundamental weakness. Yardley was driving hard, looking for runs when he should have been concentrating on survival. The chances against saving the match then must have been a thousand to one but the really experienced professional would have had a go. He would have sold himself dearly, not with his bat twirling over one shoulder.

Australia were beaten by England's professionalism. Not least, whether they like to admit it or some sections of the media recognised the fact, they were beaten on the first day when England's pros kept themselves in the game despite the odds. Australia have ability but they have a devil of a lot to learn about applying it.

There was one sad footnote to the Test. Tom Brooks announced he intended to retire and during his last afternoon in first-class cricket became involved in controversy when he gave Wood caught behind off Lever. TV replays showed that Wood had not edged the ball and some sections of the Aussie Press were quick to make him a scapegoat for the defeat. If they believe that, they will believe anything.

Tom gave years of service to cricket and it was sad to see him leaving the game under such a cloud. All umpires make mistakes and no player would pretend he doesn't resent them at the time, but players make mistakes too. The TV camera doesn't make mistakes but then it doesn't make an umpire's job any easier either. I hope Tom Brooks reconsiders his decision and gives the game the benefit of his experience again in the future.

9 Come in number 10

The wicket fell, I picked up my bat and gloves, put my cap on and was just about to set off for the middle when John Emburey went past. 'What's going on; I thought I was in next?' 'So did I, but the captain wants me in. See you.' So Emburey was at nine. I was at ten. Or was I? It was the most bizarre day of my England tour.

The three-day match against South Australia at Adelaide was attacked in the local Press as being nothing more than a practice match and we certainly took the opportunity to give the spinners a workout. The pitch was so green we considered changing the team and playing three seamers, but Emburey and Edmonds had not bowled for ages; they needed the practice. And if we had concentrated on a seam attack we could have finished the match in no time.

I don't know why the pitch had so much grass on it. Perhaps the groundsman wanted to help Hogg who, as it turned out, did not play in the match. One thing for sure – if the Test pitch is as grassy somebody will end up in hospital and the match will not last four days.

South Australia won the toss and batted, which was useful considering we would have put them in. Old bowled some superb deliveries, they could hardly put a bat on him and it was obvious we could bowl them out very cheaply if we kept the seamers on. But we gave the spinners practice and South Australia picked up far more runs than they might, thanks partly to catches which were dropped by Old, Gooch and Brearley at first slip. 'If they bowl their seamers we are going to look pretty silly by comparison,' I told Brearley. 'Probably so but the spinners do need a bowl,' he said. Despite the fact that South Australia made 241-7 declared, it was a sensible decision.

They bowled their seamers at us next morning and we got terribly bogged down. I was middling the ball well, I never played and missed once but I simply could not get it away; I did not have the confidence to attack with any determination. Lever brought a message with the drinks – get on with it! – Gooch was stumped and I was caught behind.

Tolchard played magnificently – again – and I would have put him in the Test side. He played practically every shot in the book, especially against the spinners, cutting and driving, sweeping, using his feet, pinching quick singles with Radley. It was great to watch. Radley developed confidence as the innings went on and Randall looked in super form: certainly no lack of confidence there.

We came off for a couple of showers and the light was not good, but South Australia's captain Bob Blewett agreed that if we declared they would try and stay on rather than appeal against the light. Chris Old had a migraine attack and could not bowl in any case; if they batted through we might make a game of it. So we declared at 234–5.

Emburey bowled really well in South Australia's second innings, picking up 5–67 while poor Edmonds finished with 0–91. Edmonds seemed very dispirited. After a golden year of Test cricket it was a very testing time for him.

There is always something in it for spinners at Melbourne, so Edmonds was naturally conscious of his prospects of making the third Test. Every time Emburey got a wicket I intoned 'One for Melbourne … two for Melbourne … three for Melbourne …' hoping to spur Edmonds on. In the end I said, 'You could be with me in Melbourne, Henri – on holiday.' He grinned and nodded: 'You might just be right, kid.'

To prove that the match was not altogether lighthearted the captain asked me to bowl an over before lunch. 'Where do you want your field,' he asked. 'Just put 'em where you like; they won't hit me,' I said. And it should have been a wicket maiden except that they got a single for a misfield and Tolly failed to stump Blewett down the leg side. We bowlers do suffer …

South Australia left us 239 to win in two hours plus fifteen overs. I was to bat down the order. As we left the field at lunch, Brearley asked: 'If we are chasing runs, do you want to go in first for a slog?' That is not my game and there were players in the side bursting with confidence who would make a better job of it. It seemed logical they should go in early and I should bat around seven or eight.

I was middling the ball but not striking it with any confidence. I felt too tense; perhaps the pressures of the past few months at home and on tour had got through to me. Kenny Barrington advised me to concentrate on a higher backlift; I was not picking the bat up high enough so although I was getting to the ball sweetly there was nothing there to hit it with. He advised me to play shots in the nets, to get my feet moving.

Doug Insole said he thought I had restricted myself to play in three areas, perhaps because the pitches had not been too good and I was conscious of the need not to get out early on. I was playing off my legs in front of and behind square and square on the off-side. But I was hitting nothing through mid-off or extra cover, normally a favourite area for me. The positioning was right but the strokes were stifled and truncated.

But Doug reiterated that my innings in the second Test at Perth had been crucial. He said it to cheer me up and I respected him for that.

Brearley told me I was batting at nine, perhaps to save the match if things turned out that way. He did not seem entirely convinced that we should go for a win, though Willis was all in favour of it. When the seventh wicket fell he sent in Emburey, when the ninth fell he sent in Lever above me. The dressing room thought it was great fun and I did my best to put a brave face on it but I confess I did not feel very lighthearted. I could not see the sense in it.

In form or not, I felt I had more chance of winning the match at eight or nine than tail-enders whose only hope was to slog. I accepted the principle of not going in first but it seemed crazy that I should suddenly become a number 11 batsman.

Perhaps Brearley wanted me as insurance against losing the match. I suppose I was more likely than most to stick it out if we needed to preserve the last wicket and to that extent his tactics were a compliment. But the Press were obviously going to make some capital out of it; I get more searching Press than most and I could have done without the extra pressure.

Wilfred Rhodes started his career at 11 and finished as an opener; perhaps I would merit a paragraph in the Yorkshire handbook as having progressed the other way! Perhaps I would do a Trueman if I was told to save it, smash the first ball for six and swear I was only pushing for one! I tried to laugh it off.

In the event I hit a four, we neded two to win off the last ball of the match to Miller and we got a single for a draw. One of Adelaide's more celebrated draws, I think . . .

10 Christmas cheer

Inspector Clouseau, Adam (without Eve) and of course the Queen were among the guests at England's Christmas party ...

Celebrating Christmas away from home can be a sombre experience but it's something that many cricketers have to learn to live with; and we do our best to liven the day with a fancy-dress party, a bizarre mixture of hired costumes and do-it-yourself garb. Christmas Eve was pretty quiet; we flew from Adelaide to Melbourne and did not arrive in the hotel until quite late. I watched a carol service on TV and went to bed.

Christmas Day was rather different. We traditionally have a drink with the Press in the manager's suite, then they go their own way and we get ready for our party. This year everybody was given a letter of the alphabet and had to dress accordingly; the Queen – looking remarkably like Derek Randall – swept through the foyer of the Melbourne Hilton just after lunch.

Apart from its obvious appeal, the party is an important part of team management. Some players who have toured Australia before receive private invitations to Christmas lunch; it's a nice gesture but it does mean that some newcomers to the tour might get left out. So the party is a good way of preserving and developing team togetherness.

It was a pretty motley gathering. I drew the letter A which wasn't the easiest of letters to illustrate; I finally fastened a large white towel like a nappie – there aren't too many fig-leaves in Melbourne – and wore a head band with a white flower. I looked ridiculous and I was in pretty good company.

Mike Brearley drew W and went as a warrior complete with shield and spear, Graham Gooch was Zorro, Geoff Miller went as a Derbyshire miner in baggy trousers and flat cap, John Emburey emerged as a green lizard and Bob Willis went as an umpire. Not an ordinary umpire, but a chap with a white stick and face-mask who had Fiery's Friend written across his shirt and walked about all the time with his finger in the air!

There had to be a prize for the best costume and the manager Doug Insole won that by appearing as Clouseau complete with unintelligible accent. He does it rather well. And the booby prize for the least imaginative costume went to Ian Botham, who turned up with breathtaking predictability as a gorilla ... we reminded him it was supposed to be fancy dress! It was a splendid hired costume with a hideous grinning head; it was also so hot that Both sat around with a face like a beetroot all afternoon.

Bob Willis entertained us to a recitation which would have meant absolutely nothing to an outsider but which was full of private jokes and references which had us all falling about; a casual visitor would have assumed we had taken leave of our senses. And a group of choirboys who were passing through the hotel entertained us to Christmas carols, which was a super touch.

But business is business and we had a one-day international match next day. So the captain warned us against more booze once the party finished; most of the players had a nap in the afternoon and were in bed early on Christmas Day.

11 A mild state of shock

Australia found themselves in something of a quandary at Melbourne and resolved it by dropping their offspinner Yardley. They would probably have preferred to go into the match with two front-line spinners but they also wanted to fire three seamers at us and on the evidence of their batting so far they also had to include six batsmen in the side. So Yardley had to go – but it was a decision I felt they might come to regret.

They won the toss and batted and immediately we sensed a far more positive approach from Wood and Darling. They did not slog but they were busy, alert, far more confident. They took every possible single to change the strike and our bowlers rarely got the chance to confront one batsman with half a dozen deliveries on end. Bobby Simpson and Bill Lawrie used to do that; I wondered if Simpson had been giving them some advice.

Not that Wood and Darling are in the Simpson-Lawrie class when it comes to running between the wickets. Darling backs up so far he looks as though he has already set off to run; I swear he will arrive before the ball one day. And Wood's first instinct is to strike the ball, shout: 'Yes!' and then decide whether a run is really possible. The result was a hair-raising first hour with runs coming far too quickly for our liking and at least three golden chances of a run-out. Fancy my saying that!

Darling played firmly to Randall at cover and set off, goodness knows why. Wood sensibly sent him back and Darling was still thrashing about in no-man's land when Randall's measured throw missed the stumps. The trouble was that Randall had far too much time; he did not know whether to shy at the stumps or wait for a fielder to cover them, whether to throw fast and hard or lob the ball gently. And while he was making up his mind Darling had time to check, turn and flounder back into his ground; if Randall's throw had hit, he would have been out by a mile.

Then Wood pushed and ran, was sent back and escaped by a hairsbreadth as Hendrick picked up the ball on his follow-through and rolled it underarm at the stumps. Again, Hendrick had so much time to think about it he tried too hard to make sure; Wood was still going the other way when their paths crossed!

And Australia were living dangerously again when Darling played towards Gower wide at cover and launched into a quick single. The throw missed but not by much. Considering those chances and the fact that Wood escaped a very confident appeal for bat-pad to Gower at fourth slip, Australia might have been in a familiar sort of trouble. Instead they put on 50 in seventy minutes without losing a wicket; it was far too many for our comfort.

At drinks the captain asked if we had any thoughts. It was clear we had to stem the flows of runs even if it meant putting men out and not attacking quite so fiercely. We had to bog them down or the match would get away from us.

Emburey went on and it was noticeable that both left-handers liked to get outside the offspinner, hit to mid-on or midwicket and gallop for a single. Wood got away with it once and I sensed he was looking to do it again; I moved in two or three yards at mid-on. Sure enough, Wood drove the ball straight to me, Darling was already out of his blocks and going hard when he was sent back and all I had to do was keep cool. Darling was yards out of his ground when my throw arrived and Emburey calmly took the bails off.

Perhaps there was a lesson for batsmen in that. Some fielders like Randall and Gower have a deserved reputation for brilliance; they are treated with the utmost respect. But the rest of us can do a professional job in the field, we may not be lightning but we are not past it either. I think the Aussies sometimes underestimate us.

Hughes was out to the first ball he received, an ugly-looking shot which confirmed our impressions of one of his weaknesses. He tries to go forward whenever possible, in fact he almost walks into his shots in an effort to get outside the line of the ball. The slips worry him, that's why he gets so many of his runs in the fine-leg area. The idea was to draw him wide and it was certainly a wide delivery from Botham which got him out; Hughes indicated that he hit his boot with the bat but we were sure he was caught behind. If you do hit bat against boot it is not always easy to tell if you have hit the ball as well.

At 65-2 Australia were in a delicate position, but Wood and Yallop made runs briskly, putting on 50 in just over an hour. Yallop looked in good form and his attitude was dead right; the Aussies were supposed to have some sort of a summit meeting before the Test started and it certainly seemed to be paying off for them. Yallop played the spinners particularly well, Wood made runs despite the fact that he plays practically all his shots on the leg-side. He likes to get on with it but his insistence on sweeping or working almost everything to leg restricts him a lot.

It looked ominously as though this was simply not going to be our day. They had survived the run-outs and then when he was 17 Yallop was dropped at slip by Brearley off Hendrick. It was not a difficult chance as first slips go, slightly to his right at an easily catchable height, but everyone spills one from time to time.

Yallop has a distinctive style against the seamers and Botham bowled very intelligently against him, probing for a weakness. Yallop stands up straight and drives from the back foot with very little use of his feet, usually through mid-off. Botham bowled a couple of wider deliveries and Yallop left them apprehensively, but he was tempted and, when Botham went a little wider still, he hit through the line of the ball, again without getting his foot across. Hendrick took a magnificent diving right-handed catch at second slip.

Wood had almost scored 50 by now so he was pretty well set and the pitch suited Toohey down to the ground. It was slow with very little bounce and he likes to get on to the front foot; if he played sensibly I could see us having the devil's own job to get him out. But both batsmen had fortunate escapes. Wood survived an appeal for a bat-pad catch to Botham at silly point, though we were all sure it was out, then Toohey edged Botham and Brearley dropped a straightforward chance at slip. It was hard graft and we weren't making it any easier for ourselves.

Not surprisingly the crowd was in great voice but, again, I was disappointed by a noisy, mindless minority who did their best to spoil it for the rest. They seem to congregate in sections 13 to 16 of the southern stand and I reckon most of them know a damned sight more about booze than they do about cricket. Botham, fielding close to the bat, was hit twice on the shin by Wood and Toohey and collapsed in obvious pain – and the boo-boys absolutely loved it. They seemed genuinely delighted that somebody had got hurt. I don't understand that sort of mentality or the humourless and witless foul-mouthed shouting that goes with it, but alas it seems to be increasingly common-place in Aussie cricket. Botham threw a gesture in their direction which left absolutely no doubt what he thought of them, but I thought he did well to keep his cool and bowl as thought-fully as he did.

We needed a breakthrough and Randall provided it. Wood and Toohey had put on 53 in around seventy minutes when Toohey shaped to hit Miller off his legs and got into the shot a little too early. It was firmly hit but Randall threw himself at midwicket to take a typical Randall catch – a touch of brilliance and a shrug of nonchalance to follow. 'I just stuck my hand out,' he grinned.

No Test debut is easy and Border must have felt the pressure was on him when he arrived to find four men round the bat, but he played remarkably well, using his feet adroitly and lift-ing Miller's slower ball over midwicket, not a bad shot for a man in his first Test innings. He almost gave a bat-pad chance to short square leg off the first delivery he received, but that apart he looked admirably composed.

Even so, he fell foul of the yobs when he took a single off the last ball of the penultimate over of the day. They wanted Wood to have strike so that he could reach his century before close of play and the fact that Border was batting with a rather broader concept in mind didn't impress them one bit. Wood made it just the same, driving the fourth ball of the last over straight for three while I chased hopefully, a very confident shot for a man on 97.

Australia's day without a doubt, but when you consider three run-outs that didn't quite come off and two dropped catches, it might have been very different. Australia had cursed their luck in two Test matches so far; they had no reason to complain about a total of 243–3 at the end of the day.

Second day

Nobody in his right mind could have forecast the events of the second morning. I felt Australia could bat badly and still make 350 ... and they lost their last six wickets for 15 runs in 75 minutes! It was an incredible collapse.

Brearley started it off the eighth ball of the morning with a low catch at slip as Border stretched to a widish delivery – an important breakthrough for us and a welcome relief for the captain after his misses of the day before. Confidence can be temporarily shattered, mistakes can breed mistakes, so it's always reassuring to take an early catch.

But the biggest prize was Wood, striving to dig himself in again after his century the day before. Miller normally has a fielder shortish on the off-side for the drive but he recognised that Wood is a leg-side player so he put his man on the on-side this morning. Wood was fettered and fretful; he inevitably tried his favourite shot through midwicket and gave a waist-high catch to Emburey. A nice piece of thoughtful bowling but I was surprised it hadn't occurred to Miller at some stage while he was bowling the previous day.

Australia set off like lemmings. Hogg inexplicably thumped a catch straight to cover, Dymock was crowded by fielders and got an inside edge into his stumps before he had time to establish himself, and Hurst went to his second delivery after surviving a no-ball. Hendrick, coming in downwind, was causing all sorts of panic.

Maclean battled on, determined to get a few before all his support disappeared, and Higgs clung on for a while, much to the delight and surprise of the crowd who recognise he is not the most formidable of batsmen. Botham finally replaced

Miller, chiefly to get through to Higgs, but in fact he polished off the innings at the other end when Maclean hit across the line and was bowled by a leg-stump yorker.

Australia 258 all out and you can picture how delighted we were. We never imagined they would go so cheaply, even allowing for some great bowling by Hendrick and Miller, who took three for eleven and two for two respectively in the morning. At the start of the day a crowd of 50,000 was expected, all anxious to roar Australia into a big lead; now they were sullen and subdued.

Our confidence was running high again. Of course there were pitfalls – several deliveries at the pavilion end had kept low and scurried through and that would take a bit of watching – but Yallop, Darling and Wood had made it look relatively easy. It seemed the sort of pitch on which a determined batsman could get in and score a lot of runs; I found myself talking about 450 in the first innings and a commanding lead.

And that notion fell apart inside less than three overs: seventeen deliveries to be precise. I faced twelve before I got a ball from Hogg – him again – which cut back wickedly, kept a bit low and hit my middle stump. I can't remember when I was last bowled in a Test match in Australia but I am sure somebody must have had a hernia; half the crowd did. And four deliveries after that Brearley got a similar ball and was trapped lbw; it was Perth all over again and our vision of a big lead had evaporated on a gale of hot air from 40,000 throats.

The crowd went mad and when Hogg sauntered off to field at fine leg the crowd in that area gave him a magnificent reception. They were on their feet cheering and shaking their fists, Aussie flags were waving, the din was incredible. I couldn't help reflecting that Hogg was enjoying the sort of spontaneous and genuinely-felt affection which only moments like that in real Test cricket can bring. World Series Cricket could never have given him that.

The England dressing room was in a state of mild shock, a very different place from the one Brearley and I had left together only thirty-five minutes earlier. Lunch was a very subdued affair: Randall and Gooch had a tremendous weight of responsibility and everybody in the room felt it as keenly as they did. The crowd were baying and cheering, lifting Hogg with every stride, it was like batting against 40,000 bowlers at each end.

They braved it out, grafting hard, but just when it seemed they had ridden the worst of the storm Randall was out lbw to Hurst. He eyed the umpire quizzically for some seconds, but I think he thought he was further over than he really was. The delivery swung and dipped into him as he went across and outside the off stump; he tried to get back with his left foot but he simply could not find the room.

Gooch had been in for almost two hours, fighting hard and cover-driving Hogg stylishly to suggest he was almost settled in, when Dymock flushed him out with a delivery which was angled across him and bounced a little. He got an edge and Border took a fine catch at second slip, juggling at first and then clutching the ball to his body as he fell. At 52–4 we were still in real trouble, especially since Dymock was bowling well, doing a really professional job of containment which allowed Hogg to have a rest without blunting the Aussie attack.

Inexplicably, Yallop brought on Higgs for Hurst. The quicker bowler had been on for a fair spell but if he needed a rest I thought it would have made more sense to switch Dymock and bring back Hogg. As it was, Gower stole a few runs off Higgs and that relieved the pressure a little – not much but enough to give us a fractional breathing space. Gower and Botham put on 23; we were 75–4 at tea.

The pitch accounted for Gower. He was trapped lbw by a delivery from Dymock which pitched and skidded through without bouncing – and England were in a state of crisis again. Our last two recognised batsmen, Botham and Miller, were at the crease, the score was only 81 and Hogg was ready to come back into the firing line after a long rest. It really was a desperate situation.

As if that was not enough, the crowd took a special dislike to Botham. An article claiming to be an exclusive interview with Botham had appeared in a sports paper, rubbishing the Australian team and spectators and generally crowing about England's success in two Tests. It totally misrepresented Botham's attitude, making him sound like an intolerable braggart; the sort of inflammatory, provocative nonsense which no cricketer in his right mind would say. It certainly did not reflect Both's attitude but the crowd were waiting for him, jeering and slow handclapping from the moment he showed his face. That's the sort of extra pressure batsmen can do without – I should know.

Dymock bowled as tightly as ever, Higgs's field was set deep and it was fearfully hard to find a run. Botham began to fret, winding at both bowlers without connecting, and Miller was in trouble, missed at slip, which was rather too wide. Yet, desperate as England's predicament was, Higgs bowled to only one slip – an extraordinary piece of captaincy. Higgs should have had three or four men round the bat, especially since the odd delivery bounced or turned a little or kept low. Miller often played outside the line and the ball bobbled off bat and pad, yet there were no close fielders to take advantage or turn the pressure on fully. England could not score but in their situation they should have been under the fiercest pressure from men round the bat; Yallop seemed happy to contain us.

Having said that, Botham and Miller did not help themselves a great deal. They did not talk together enough when the situation cried out for some sort of concerted plan, an exchange of ideas and suggestions. With Higgs's fields so deep they might have decided to look for singles off him to push the score along; instead Miller seemed to be trying to play his way out of trouble and Botham looked as though he wanted to hit his way clear. There was an obvious lack of cohesion.

Botham leg-glanced Dymock and cover-drove him magnificently for four. And in the midst of the crisis he suddenly unleashed an incredible shot over mid-off for two, the sort of thing he might normally produce in the thirty-ninth over of a Sunday League match. When Hogg came back Botham hooked him powerfully for four but even Botham can live dangerously for only so long. He drove Higgs uppishly into the covers, Darling threw himself forward for the catch and England were 100–6.

Taylor went quickly, bowled off his right pad by a delivery which kept low, and Hogg became the avenging hero once again. The crowd spurred him on, Hogg raced in and Emburey did well to withstand the pressure for a quarter of an hour. Three deliveries from Hogg just about summed up the difficulties batsmen were under: the first lifted chest-high as he played back, the second skidded and hit the bottom of his bat as he played forward and the third was up round his chest again. Finally a delivery of full length scuttled straight under his bat; not much anyone can do about those.

The fall of Botham and two quick wickets for Hogg had masked Yallop's failure to turn the screw with Higgs. England were 107-8 and Yallop would have settled for that at the start of the day. Hogg was asked why he does so well against us and said: 'I just bowl straight to hit. If you bowl wide these English so-and-sos leave it, they won't hook or pull.' It struck me that his style and attitude – an awkward length, a good line and the ability to cut the ball back – were very reminiscent of Brian Statham.

Hogg is rather more volatile than Statham, no doubt about that. Yallop had a bit of trouble with him in the last half hour or so when Miller and Willis were hanging on for all they were worth. 'Funny feller this Hogg,' said Willis later. 'Every time I go in to bat he wants to be taken off ...' The dressing room needed a bit of light relief.

Third day

Mike Brearley knows a thing or two about the value of positive thinking so there was no mistaking his message before play started: we still have a chance of winning the match. He reasoned that if we could bowl them out for 150 or 180 and then bat well we could still swing the game; if we did not bowl them out we must make sure they struggled for runs. We had to take wickets or absorb time so we would not have too long to bat to save the match if necessary – it was simple, positive and straight to the point.

We got an unexpected bonus early on when the tail-enders batted on for an hour and made another 35 invaluable runs, but we knew we would have to bowl and field well to stay in the match. 'Don't give them anything to cut or hook', was the golden rule and Botham, over-pitching slightly in his anxiety to keep the ball up to the bat, was chipped for ones and twos.

Wood and Darling made a confident start despite the inevitable death wish when Darling played the ball straight at Gower at cover and escaped being run out by a fraction. The Aussies' lead of 115 was growing too fast and too easily for our liking.

The field became more defensive, the batsmen began to struggle and twenty-five minutes after lunch we knew we had bottled them up because some of the crowd started to slow handclap. Darling played a shot which reeked of frustration, trying to hit Miller through cover off the back foot, and Randall took the catch low down.

After his first-ball dismissal in the first innings Hughes was determined to play his shots, straight-driving and glancing Botham for four. But Wood was bogged down, nagged to death by the offspinner from one end and seamers bowling with the wind from the other. Hendrick is magnificent in a situation like this – the ball is never quite up and never short, there is absolutely nothing to hit; he drives batsmen to distraction.

Australia were 81–2 when Wood fell to Botham. He read the slower ball quickly, tried to get right outside the line to sweep and the ball flicked his pad before hitting leg stump.

For all his aggressive intentions, Hughes was made to struggle. He got very well forward and played some magnificently-struck shots but straight at fielders – and that is probably more frustrating for a batsman than not playing shots at all. With the constant fear of a shooter it was important to play forward as much as possible, but that cut out a wide range of shots; the only back-foot shots batsmen could risk were against deliveries short and wide and our bowlers made sure they did not serve up many of those. They bowled very straight, wicket to wicket; there were no cheap runs about.

Hughes finally broke out with a clonk over midwicket off Emburey. It was a good shot but the fact that he played it at all showed how anxious he was to squeeze runs from somewhere. It was mean cricket, tense and tight, competitive and highly pressurised. Just what Test cricket is about. The real, the ultimate game – England v. Australia.

Yallop was out just before tea. He went forward to a delivery from Miller, found it was a bit shorter than he expected and was trying to cut when he got an underside edge.

Bob Taylor did the rest and Australia were 101–3.

Brearley decided to mount an all-spin attack after tea and while I appreciate that any captain has to back his judgement I would not have interfered with the bowling pattern at that stage. Hughes wasn't exactly steaming along, there was a new batsman at the crease and the blend of spin and seam had served us well throughout the afternoon. Miller and Emburey have different styles but they are both offspinners presenting basically the same problem to batsmen. Batting against one is practice for facing the other.

Hughes suddenly cut loose, lofting Miller for a huge six and belting Emburey to the pavilion for four; Toohey edged three through a vacant slip area and picked up ones and twos off his legs. In half an hour they put on thirty runs, which was a lot – too many – in a low-scoring match like this. Hendrick came back to bowl his nerve-grinding length and restore the pressure, although he was in some difficulty himself. His throat was bone dry and he could not make any saliva; the umpire Max O'Connell carried a small spray and used it on Hendo's throat at the end of every over.

Toohey was working the spinners so effectively that we adjusted the close legside field to try and slow him down a bit, but he still made 20 in no time. The depth of the defensive field finally proved his undoing; he tried to hit extra hard to pierce it and Botham took a good catch diving forward at midwicket. The crowd had enjoyed themselves tremendously at Both's expense when he was hit at short leg, so his remarks when he took the catch were suitably colourful.

Border, who almost played on to Emburey and never looked comfortable, was dismissed by a brilliant blend of reflex and accuracy by Hendrick at backward short leg. Border mistimed a sweep, lost his balance and was trying desperately to regain his equilibrium and his ground when Hendo scooped the ball on to his stumps. It all happened in a flash; I don't suppose Hendrick had more than a couple of seconds to react.

Australia had suddenly lost two wickets without scoring a run, Hughes was fretting and I sensed that he intended to whack Botham if the ball was pitched up to him. As Botham walked back to his mark I called over: 'Bowl as straight as possible and bowl Hendo's length or he will clonk it.' As Botham let it go Hughes tried to charge him, but because the delivery was a bit shorter than he expected he never really got to it and Gower took a catch waist-high. If the ball had been pitched up it would have gone many a mile.

Botham's tail was up and the fact that the yobs in the crowd were having a go only made him more combative. They went mad as he walked towards them, yelling and swearing, a forest of V signs, and Both grinned and nodded as though they were on his side! Hogg came in without a helmet and that was quite enough to persuade Botham a bouncer was needed. By the time it reached Hogg it was travelling at about ten miles per hour and fading fast, a real lollipop of a delivery. Big grins all round.

The light wasn't good and since Botham was steaming in I thought the Aussies were unfortunate to have an appeal against the light turned down. Hogg seemed to be trying to turn a full-length delivery through midwicket when it hit his off stump about ten inches off the ground, and although Maclean hung on gamely with men round the bat he was obviously having the greatest difficulty picking the ball up in the gloom.

Australia finished the day on 163–7, a lead of 278. I thought it was a fascinating day's cricket but as I was going back to the hotel I was accosted by a guy who looked distinctly the worse for wear. 'Rubbish cricket today, mate. Not enough runs,' he said. Anything more subtle than a six or a can of ale was obviously lost on him.

Fourth day
If we could knock over their tail quickly we had a chance of winning the match – but it was a tall order and we were under no illusions. The pitch was at its worst; back-foot shots were virtually impossible and runs were terribly difficult to come by – and we were thinking in terms of making the highest score of the match batting last to win. It doesn't happen often in any cricket match, least of all in a Test match.

We decided against taking the new ball even though it was available, because Maclean had looked vulnerable against the spinners and we felt we could get through quicker with a spinner on. Maclean was soon out sweeping and their innings was polished off by a fine stumping when Higgs pushed well forward and was beaten by Emburey. Australia 167 all out, and we could hardly have done much better than that in the circumstances: we had done remarkably well and yet we would have to do even better if we were to score 283 to win. We had time – almost two days – but that also meant Australia had a long time to pressurise us if they got on top.

Still, there was a fair amount of optimism in the dressing room that we would do it. Why not? We were two up in the series, we had outplayed Aussie before. As long as we played forward whenever possible and kept our heads there was a feeling we could pull it off.

As a realist, even an optimistic one, I felt we would win only if somebody made a century. Others would have to chip in but it was vital that the innings had the backbone of at least one major individual score. And it was also important that we scored at least eighty runs before the second wicket went down; one of the openers might go early against the new ball but it was imperative we did not lose a wicket for some time after that. Hogg had invariably taken wickets early with the new ball and it was vital to block him out.

The Aussies soon made it clear just how difficult it was going to be. They started talking – not to Mike Brearley or myself, of course, but across us from silly point to short square leg; Yallop and Higgs in a sort of double act which was clearly intended to intimidate. 'Look at the holes ... be in terrible trouble if it pitches there ... that was lucky ... didn't know much about that, did he ... he's a lucky so-and-so this one ...' and so on.

Between deliveries from Hogg Yallop shuffled forward on to the cut area of the pitch. He was so close we could hear each other breathing; he stared at me, I stared back, rather like that game which kids play to see who will look away first. Then he sang out, 'Come on Hoggy, let's have a really quick one.' Intimidation, gamesmanship, call it what you like; and the innings had barely started.

At the end of the over I had a word with umpire, Max O'Connell. 'They're giving you a bit of verbal, aren't they,' said Max. 'I moved quite a bit closer and I could hear something was going on.' I said I was pretty used to it after a few years in Test cricket – 'I don't mind it too much as long as they don't talk while I'm actually facing.' O'Connell said he would watch the situation and gave his partner the wink.

We were in trouble almost immediately. Brearley drove at a wide one and was caught behind, and Randall fell lbw to a delivery which pitched off stump and hit just below the knee roll as he tried to work it on the on-side. There was a suspicion that it might have done too much but the umpire thought otherwise.

One or two deliveries kept low, I blocked them out and Wood remarked: 'You must be really worried about them.' 'Why's that?' 'Well, you're not in very good form, are you; you're just struggling along.' It wasn't exactly intended as a reassurance. Added to that sort of thing, Hogg was dancing about like a madman every time the ball hit the pad and the crowd were roaring every delivery. Quite a torrid time.

Gooch and I got through to lunch, defending when we had to and playing a few pleasing shots – a cover drive for four off Dymock and a four off the back foot against Higgs for Gooch; a couple of leg glances off Hogg and Hurst from me. But just before lunch Gooch played forward to Higgs, the ball turned appreciably and we ran three byes; very ominous.

I thought Yallop would persevere with Higgs after lunch because of the way that delivery turned and the fact that the cracks and holes in the pitch weren't exactly getting any narrower. With Higgs on and men round the bat we would have been under real pressure. Instead he had Dymock bowling round the wicket and Gooch picked up runs with a drive and a wider delivery slashed for four.

Gooch had braved it out for ninety-seven minutes when he was beaten by Hogg's most formidable delivery, the one which he brings back sharply from outside the off stump. He was playing forward, and I think the ball would have hit middle stump but probably his foot was outside the off stump. Hogg brought one back at me soon afterwards which almost cut me in half, but the real danger man should have been Higgs, who was making the ball lift and turn alarmingly. We dared not drive unless the ball was pitched right up to the bat; when we tried to play off the back foot the ball kept low and we simply banged it into the ground and yet Higgs bowled with only one slip and nobody round the bat to pressurise us. It was inexplicable.

Gower and I talked to each other a lot, swapping ideas, keeping ourselves in the game. I told him the important thing was to play a responsible innings and that he should get forward whenever possible. Aussie began to get a bit rattled and I reckon that if Gower and I had been together forty minutes after tea we would have had them panicking; as it was they were beginning to look a little frayed round the edges.

But I got out in the last over before tea. I had batted for 198 minutes – the longest innings in the side as it turned out – when I played well forward to a delivery from Hurst intending to hit through midwicket. It kept low, hit me on the lower part of the shin and that was that. Apart from Maclean telling me to F*** off, of course.

The yobs booed themselves hoarse as I walked off, though I noticed that the majority of spectators round the ground gave me a good reception. I don't mind the yobs booing, it usually means we are doing OK, but it makes me sad to think they jeer because they do not know what they are watching.

Hogg and Hurst both went round the wicket to Gower, which troubled him quite a bit; he played and missed and escaped when Hurst brought one back from eighteen inches outside off stump which ricocheted off the bat handle. But he and Botham made a fight of it – seventy-eight minutes for twenty-one runs together – before Botham pushed forward to a delivery which turned and Maclean took a good catch standing up. Half the side was out for 163, our chances of saving the match were already negligible and they disappeared completely in the next twenty minutes.

Dymock had one big shout for lbw against Gower turned down, but the next delivery pitched just outside off stump and would have hit middle had Gower not got his pad in the way. Then Miller was caught at short square leg off bat and pad as he tried to turn a delivery from Higgs. Taylor braved it out for forty minutes, but a few minutes before the close he groped for a wide one off Hogg and was caught behind. At 171–8, the last day was just a matter of polishing off the innings and it was all over in twenty-five minutes – but not without an incident which left Bob Willis fuming, and rightly so.

Willis received a bouncer from Hogg, played it with his glove in front of his face and was caught at short leg. He is not supposed to face bouncers and what annoyed him even more was the memory of Pakistan at Edgbaston last year when he was strongly criticised for felling the nightwatchman Qasim. 'Just because I get a glove in the way nothing is said. But if the ball had hit me in the face there would have been hell on. It was the same sort of delivery, where's the justice in that,' said Willis. It had been settled between the two captains before the match that the last two batsmen – Hendrick and Willis in England's case – should be exempt from bouncers. No wonder Bob Willis was angry.

I do believe that we have not yet settled the bouncer problem.

Australia won by 103 runs and the result was widely hailed as a good thing for cricket. We set out to win and there's not the slightest doubt we would have reversed the result if we could, but on reflection I can understand the reaction. Australians are good winners but not very happy losers; they like to be associated with success and it had been suggested that another England victory would have signalled the death of traditional cricket in Australia. They won on merit and it would be interesting to see how that affected their attitude in the Tests to come.

Mike Brearley lost his first Test as captain and that is bound to have some sort of effect on him; perhaps winning a Test will be the boost Yallop needs but I still cannot rate him highly as a skipper. Even when we were up against it he was reluctant to attack strongly or put us under extreme pressure; he kept plugging away with seamers and hoped something would happen. The only time he attacked was when he was sure he could not lose and the fear of defeat rather than an ambition for victory seems to sway his judgement.

The Aussies grumbled a bit about some decisions at Perth but they could have no complaints now; there were seven lbw decisions in the match and they all went against England!

Wood was selected as Man of the Match and after scores of 100 and 34 on that pitch he deserved it, but he could have been out early, and had that happened the match might have gone quite differently. He got into hot water for his outspoken criticism of the umpiring at Perth but, like all batsmen, he didn't say too much about the decisions which went his way at Melbourne. I am waiting for a batsman to be quoted in the Press saying: 'That was a terrible decision; I was definitely out ...' That'll be the day.

12 Off the hook

Whatever happened to Phil Edmonds? We named the same twelve for the fourth Test in Sydney, though with the greatest respect to Emburey and Miller I would have preferred to see Edmonds in the squad for the sake of balance. Trouble is, Edmonds was very low in spirit, he had not bowled much and he needed someone or something to pick him up and to get him bowling with enthusiasm again.

There wasn't much time for practice between the Tests and the practice we had was of very limited value. The nets were hopeless and Australia's wicketkeeper John Maclean was hit above the eye by a delivery which lifted from a length; there was some doubt about his fitness to play but he was eventually declared fit. World Series players had been practising in the nets for some time and they were badly over-used; the spinners could turn the ball square and seamers had to bowl off three or four paces to avoid injury to batsmen. Unfortunately most of the net pitches – and come to think of it, the Test pitches as well so far – hadn't been very good either.

That can make quite a difference. We discussed the problems posed by Hogg at a team talk and Ken Barrington said we should be looking to play forward despite his turn of speed. I agreed, but that isn't easy when net surfaces have been so poor and batsmen are tentative because of the state of pitches. Good nets breed confidence in batsmen and we were not over-brimming with that. But it was obvious that we must keep Hogg out early on; he was their danger man and without him they were not half as effective as a bowling side.

I also pointed out that their openers, Wood and Darling, were getting runs far too quickly. They are both nervous players early on and we should try to close them down and frustrate them, prevent them snatching singles. Wood is a leg-

The face of Australian cricket in 1979. Rodney Hogg, for me unarguably the man of the series.

On my way to 123 not out at Canberra.

The first wicket of the Ashes series: Gary Cosier run-out by a throw from David Gower.

Going ... going ... I am run out in the second innings.

An early blow: Graham Gooch caught by John Maclean off Hogg for one.

Jubilation for Australia as Hurst traps me lbw for 77 at Perth.

Ouch! David Gower hit on the ear-shield by a delivery from Rodney Hogg.

Peter Toohey opens up and Ian Botham – crash helmet or not – has to duck.

After the victory – Botham, myself, Emburey, Taylor, Lever, Miller and an unidentified fan find time to celebrate.

A pensive moment for me in the third Test.

A little extra bounce, an error of judgement and I am caught by Alan Border off Alan Hurst for eight at Sydney.

The Ashes retained. Alan Hurst edges a delivery from Emburey into his stumps and we have won the fourth Test.

A stroke I enjoyed as David Gower looks on appreciatively.

It is not generally known that I have taken more wickets for my country than for Yorkshire. I was used as an occasional bowler on this tour. Four overs in four months. Very occasional.

Dennis Lillee bowling at a 'Supertest' in Melbourne.

England Touring team, Australia 1978-79.

side player so the attack should be directed outside his off stump. Yet Botham, bowling round the wicket at him had a tendency to get impatient and bowl close to off stump; the swing of the ball into him then allowed Wood to work it on the leg-side. So Botham would have to be more patient. Darling likes to hit and run; I thought we should have a mid-off in after the first few overs.

Brearley won the toss for the first time in the series and elected to bat on a pitch which was soon seen to be two-paced. Some deliveries kept low, others went through really quickly; one smacked Brearley under the heart and, had he not been wearing chest protection, it would have caved his ribs in. Once Hogg saw it would bounce he whacked the ball in, then varied his deliveries a lot as we kept him out. Dymock swung a couple and bowled a superb delivery to me which swung in, pitched middle-and-off, and seamed away. 'If we can keep them out until lunch this will be a good toss to win,' I said and Brearley nodded.

I had batted for almost an hour when Hurst got me out, caught chest-high by Border at second slip. I was surprised by the bounce – it hadn't been particularly untoward up to then – but the ball was still going up when it reached Border and he took it with both hands. Two deliveries later we were in trouble again.

Randall hooked his second ball from Hurst and hit it well, square off the bat, a fine shot except that he hit it straight at Wood who was fielding at leg gully. The ball almost knocked Wood over as he threw up his hands to protect his face, but he palmed it upwards and kept his head, despite losing his balance, to take a super catch.

Brearley played a couple of controlled drives against Dymock and seemed to be pretty well set, when Hogg came back into the attack and beat him with a very fine delivery. It swung in a little and Mike shaped to push through mid-on, but the ball pitched off stump, held up as he played across the line and hit off stump. England were at an uncomfortable 35–3.

Hurst, bowling round the wicket at Gower, seemed to be able to bowl wide of the off stump and still make the ball go into Gower's body – and I suspect Bobby Simpson has put

Australia up to that. They now seem to realise that if they give Gower any room to work outside the off stump he will drive powerfully or cut well, so they concentrate on tucking him up. Just when we needed consolidation and a major innings, Gower was out to the last ball before lunch.

He looked as though he intended to play forward but stayed back as a delivery from Hurst followed him, decided to leave it but didn't get his arms and bat out of the way. He should have shouldered arms, but the ball took the merest flick of his glove and went through to Maclean. Gower took an involuntary step forward to walk and that may have cost him his wicket; the umpire took a long time to give him out, there was obviously the suspicion of a doubt in his mind and Gower's reaction may have tilted the scales. What was certain was that England were 51–4 at lunch and struggling.

Yallop brought on Higgs after lunch, probably because he dismissed Botham twice in Melbourne. Hogg was still bowling quick against a very determined Gooch and when Botham got to his end he was greeted with the inevitable bouncer; Ian replied with a Chinese cut for two and a hook off the splice for a single! Hogg bowled the last ball of his over off a short run – I get the impression he prefers six-ball to eight-ball overs; it seems altogether too much hard work for him to bowl eight deliveries in succession off his full run . . .

Gooch was pressurised with men at short square on both sides of the bat; it was tight cricket in a testing situation and when Higgs dropped one short Gooch banged it to deep mid-wicket, where Toohey took a superb sliding catch. That was poor thinking on Gooch's part: even under pressure he could have hit that delivery practically anywhere.

Already I could feel the match slipping away from us. The crowd felt that they were on top; the Australians were lifted by the cheering and chanting, and we were struggling to stay afloat. They even knocked twenty minutes off the regulation period and took drinks at 2.20 pm, goodness knows why. And when Miller edged a catch low to Maclean we were 70–6 and in desperate trouble.

Maclean had to go off in mid-afternoon. He felt groggy, his vision was impaired and it turned out that a mixture of the heat and antibiotics he was taking after his eye injury in the nets had overcome him. Yallop took over behind the stumps and made a very competent job of it.

Botham hit Higgs for four off the back foot after batting for seventy-five minutes, his first boundary, which was a considerable feat of patience for him. He was clearly chafing at the bit but he stuck it well and so did Taylor. They put on twenty-three, the best stand of the innings, before Taylor pushed at a wide one from Higgs which turned and steered it to gully. Botham, impatient, got annoyed when Australia fielded their substitute Yardley in a specialist position at gully and insisted, quite rightly, that he had to be moved. Dymock retorted with a bouncer and Botham hooked it off the splice for a single, then Emburey poked a delivery straight into Higgs's midriff at short leg and was dropped. Quite an eventful over.

Emburey went soon afterwards, popping a simple catch to short square leg, but Willis lurched his long left leg down the pitch, played for survival and let Botham pick up runs at the other end. It was quite a contest, with Botham driving Dymock off back and front foot for four, cutting Higgs and pulling and driving Hogg for boundaries. His sheer strength means he can get runs off nicks and edges and when he sent a hook skittling through fine leg for four Hogg had a few choice words to say. The next ball was a slow yorker – good thinking – and the one after that was a bouncer wide of the off stump. Botham accepted the challenge, mis-hooked to the wicketkeeper and had to suffer the extra indignity of a two-handed V sign from Hogg as he walked away. Hendrick was yorked and by 5.40 pm we were all out for 152.

We made a great start in the field when Wood was out fourth ball. He looked as though he intended to duck under a short delivery, realised it wasn't short enough and dragged it on as he played a hasty shot. But neither Willis nor Botham looked very formidable; there was little real pace or sparkle and Aussie picked up all their runs off short-pitched deliveries.

It was soon obvious that Willis was struggling and about thirty minutes from the end he finished an over off a shortened run and then left the field. Clive Radley took him back to the hotel.

I noticed that Botham was not as quick at Perth or Melbourne as he was at Brisbane in the first Test; he had dropped to medium pace. He was likely to be a bit sweaty and jaded after his batting stint and I would not have given him the new ball; nobody had shown the ability to bowl tight and accurately more consistently than Hendrick and with our small total it was essential Australia did not get a runaway start. But we were never in control until Hendo clamped down with two fine overs and Australia had raced to 56–1 at the close.

It was a dreadful day for England, the worst since the opening match of the tour at Adelaide and at least we had some excuse then. There was no excuse at all now; we simply never got into the game. In the first two Tests we were well on top, then we lost the third and now they looked a beter team. It was an ominous thought.

Second day

Brearley rightly left nobody in any doubt that our performance had to improve and Mike Hendrick suggested that nobody was really pushing himself to the limit. It was not that players weren't trying – that would be a ridiculous suggestion – but rather that they were not pulling the last ounce of effort and concentration out of themselves. Perhaps going two-up in the series had made us slightly lazy. But we were not despondent, in fact we still reckoned if we could bowl them out for a lead of not more than a hundred we were in with a chance of winning the match: Tests at Sydney tend traditionally to be low scoring.

We opened with Hendrick, the man who can attack batsmen without giving them anything to hit. The few runs they scored early on came from pushes and edges; there was nothing resembling a long hop or half volley. Botham also hit a good line and length from the start, bowling with a much more positive attitude. Australia got off to a slow start which was the way we wanted it.

It was stiflingly hot and seam bowlers got little relief from a stiffish breeze, even though they had to run into it from one end. So they needed careful handling and Brearley soon had Emburey on. He bowled one bad over to Darling – who will pull anything slightly short of a length – but apart from that he was accurate and impressive. Willis bowled off a shortened run because he was still not feeling completely fit and in fact he bowled better for it; his line was better and the ball came through more convincingly. Australia struggled and we felt the match was not running away from us as it had threatened to do the previous evening.

But they were still winning it by degrees, even if those spectators who broke into a slow handclap from time to time didn't seem to appreciate the fact. At lunch they were 126–1, a good morning session without losing a wicket, and they had all the time in the world – which made Hughes's dismissal hard to explain. He slashed hard on the up at a widish delivery from Willis and was caught at cover off the first ball after the interval. An unnecessary way to go.

Bob Willis finally had to give it up and go back to the hotel. He had spent a restless night suffering from a virus infection which was aggravated by the heat and he did well to stay on as long as he did. That was bad enough but later in the afternoon Mike Hendrick had to go off, too. He was dehydrated, said he had stomach cramps and felt sick. So we lost two major bowlers just when the bowling had to be at its most accurate: a very heavy blow.

Botham stepped into the breach. We had never doubted his fierce competitiveness nor his appetite for hard work but his performance in the oppressive heat under a heavy responsibility was magnificent. There is no bigger-hearted player in the game. He was not particularly fast – the ball was far too old for that – but he put every ounce of himself into his bowling and that's a fair amount of strength and energy.

Darling had looked frustrated for some time, taking two huge swipes at Hendrick as the pressure mounted. He likes to score his runs quickly and on that surface he did not have the range of shots to do it against tight bowling. He had slowed on his way into the nineties and was nine runs from a century when Botham caught him low down at backward short leg. Toohey came in to a great reception from the Hill who had unofficially named their bar the Peter Toohey Stand – but scored only one run before Botham had him caught at slip. The return journey must have seemed endless.

Australia were 179-4 and Brearley urged the lads on. 'Two more wickets and we have opened them up,' he said; and to give Botham an added incentive he grinned, 'Two more wickets, Both, and your mate Hoggy's in ...' Botham snorted. but even he could not bowl too long in that heat, his energy had to be conserved and Brearley took him off, switching Emburey and bringing Miller on. It was a shrewd move in view of our depleted bowling resources because it gave the batsmen something new to think about at both ends, but Yallop is a good player of spin however well it is bowled and he got away from us with boundaries off both bowlers.

Hendrick came back on the field so as to be available to take the new ball and although he did not really feel up to it he got Yallop out to a superb catch by Botham, low and two-handed at slip. We still had two hours to go and despite the permutations we had tried there was still the problem of not over-bowling the men who might do most damage, so Brearley put Gooch on at one end and alternated Hendrick or Botham downwind.

It served its purpose, but at drinks Brearley asked me what I thought and I said we must replace Gooch with one of the offspinners. I said that because it seemed clear that Border had Gooch's measure and was ready to start taking runs off him. He was hitting the ball confidently and hard and as soon as he started piercing the field he could run up twenty or thirty in no time. So Emburey was brought back.

Maclean looked in terrible trouble, in fact he had struggled against the offspinners in his two previous innings. He likes to sweep, but that had got him out so often he dared not do it; he loves to cut but they gave him nothing wide of the off stump. And because this was a Test situation he dared not resort to his third alternative – as he most certainly would in Grade cricket – and have a mighty slog for runs. Batsmen who get out slogging in Test matches are frowned upon. So he really did not have a stroke to offer with confidence and, inevitably, he played back to a half volley and was lbw.

Hogg did not last long. He got off the mark with a good four over midwicket off Emburey but then became involved in an horrendous run-out. Border pushed the ball in front of square leg and set off; Hogg tried to send him back because he saw Gower swooping in, but Border was definitely on his way. Hogg did not know whether to run or refuse and both batsmen were running the same way for a second; the confusion was so total that although Gower's underarm throw at the wicket missed there was still time for Miller to lob the ball to Taylor at the other end and run Hogg out.

Australia finished the day 248-7, a lead of 96, and considering our position at the start of the day and difficulties during it we had done exceptionally well. It was good to see the team really competing again and looking more like the side which has done well, though how much good it will do us in terms of the result still remain to be seen. We would have to bat like supermen.

Fielding had been quite an experience. Six hours standing in front of the Hill is like fielding in a parrot's cage or standing in the middle of Piccadilly Circus; the noise is interminable, fights break out as the fans succumb to a mixture of hot sun and cold beer; most of the catcalls are abusive and very few are funny any more.

The last hour is the worst because by then the beer is talking. I was pelted with eggs, oranges, gherkins, nuts, ice cubes and various other bits of debris and the area was suddenly covered with seagulls queueing up for a free meal. The abuse became more drunken and vitriolic, though to be fair some voices did shout apologies for the rest: 'We're not all like that, Geoff ...' I do hope not.

There was a tap on my shoulder and suddenly I was confronted by this enormous shape. I thought for a minute one of Packer's floodlights had lurched forward on to the ground; he must have been almost seven feet tall and weighed at least twenty stone. He stuck out a hand like a dustbin lid and asked me to swap my England cap for a bright green creation he was carrying with him, but I managed to save my cap by jamming his on top of it. The Hill showed their approval by lobbing a few empty beer cans and cheering madly; they were in a dangerous mood so when Hogg was out and several of them ran on for autographs I signed a few.

When I got off the field Kenny Barrington told me the

trustees of the ground had objected to my signing autographs on the field. I don't exactly make a practice of signing autographs on the field but I did what I did to try and keep the Hill happy when they were in a potentially dangerous mood. It annoyed me that people who did not have to face an awkward physical situation should condemn my actions out of hand. It was on the cards that an ugly situation could have arisen – I had only tried to draw the sting out of a difficult situation – and I think the Hill, by and large, appreciated my actions which cooled things down. Poor Kenny Barrington had to face the complaint – and it certainly wasn't his fault.

Third day

We needed Australia out quickly but the early signs weren't too promising; Botham and Hendrick could not break through and Emburey bowled well without any luck, having Dymock dropped at silly point by Brearley. The bouncer problem cropped up again when Botham bowled one at Dymock and umpire Robin Bailhache told him to cut it out. Botham was angry, Brearley was angry – after all Dymock had been in for over an hour – but the umpire insisted it was his responsibility to decide whether or when a batsman could receive bouncers. There was obviously a misunderstanding between the umpires and the English captain as to the interpretation of the bouncer agreement – and the position is far from satisfactory and needs to be clarified by the authorities so that such misunderstandings cannot occur in the future.

Inevitably, Botham's next delivery was just short of a length, there was more argy-bargy and then Botham stuck one in about two yards faster and bowled Dymock neck and crop. The crowd booed; Botham gave them a two-handed salute of triumph – or something.

We put the field back for Border so that he could barely find a run and although Higgs hung around for some time – partly because Hendrick and Botham were jaded – he is not exactly the quickest of scorers. He scored quicker than Border, which shows just how slow their progress rate was, until he fenced at Hendrick and gave a simple catch.

Border got the slow handclap from the crowd, hit Emburey through extra cover for four and was then involved in another run-out fiasco. Both he and Hurst had made up their minds to run but unfortunately Border had forgotten to mention the fact to his partner! Border pushed the ball back down the pitch to Miller and set off; Hurst was going just as hard and just as inexplicably and Miller had only to pick the ball up on his follow-through and roll it on to the wicket.

Australia finished with a lead of 142. They had batted for a hundred minutes but without slogging us around nearly as freely as they must have hoped; as far as we were concerned it was a job well done.

There was a brief panic in the dressing room. As I picked up a pad to get ready the strap flicked me in the left eye and dislodged a contact lens; it flew out and Barrington and Gower crawled about on their hands and knees looking for it while Randall prepared himself to go in first if necessary. Finally the lens was found and replaced ... so that I could face one ball!

It was a loosener from Hogg, a little medium-pacer bowled off an exploratory run. I played well forward, it nipped back a lot and hit my front pad; I wasn't concerned when they appealed because they always do but I was astounded when I was given out by a delivery which I felt sure would have missed leg stump.

More than that – and there is no point in pretending otherwise – I was inwardly furious. It was not the first bad lbw decision we had suffered in the series. Although you try to be philosophical, umpires, particularly at top level, have an extremely difficult job and I have never lost sight of that, but sympathising with them does not help them or us. Unfortunately the lbw law seems to be interpreted differently in the various parts of the world, and this makes it difficult for both batsmen and bowlers to plan their strategy and techniques.

The Australian Press had set me up as Public Enemy Number One and it seemed there was no length to which the Aussie team would not go to get me out. I was tired of their everlasting appealing – not just against me but against every batsman in the team. They were hopping about congratulating themselves and I was – still am – convinced that I had been given out unfairly. It happens to everyone and nobody likes it; but it seems to happen far too often these days.

Hogg soon switched ends, bowling in harness with Dymock, but the pitch was good, Randall was in control and runs came quite freely. Yallop swapped and changed his bowlers through the day but he could not alter a steady pattern: frustration for Australia and measured progress by Randall and Brearley. At tea we were 74–1, slow going perhaps, but we weren't exactly in a position to take risks.

Randall took his responsibilities seriously, so much so that he became becalmed in the evening and Brearley caught him up. Hogg raced in during a late spell when he tried desperately hard to force a breakthrough, but both batsmen kept their heads down and eventually saw him off. But just when it seemed that the partnership would last out the day, Brearley was bowled by Border for 53.

Border is an innocuous sort of bowler who doesn't spin the ball much – 'It revolves twice during its trip down the pitch,' says Brearley – but the one which took the wicket pitched middle and leg and turned enough to flick away the off bail. Brearley shaped to play on the on-side and wicketkeeper Maclean moved outside the leg stump in anticipation. It was one right out of the blue.

We finished the day nine runs behind on 133–2 and Brearley said, quite rightly, that we had done a good professional job in pulling ourselves together after the horrors of the first day. We looked like a Test side again. Perhaps nobody exemplified the attitude better than Randall, who batted four hours for 60, hardly the way he would choose to play an innings. Most un-Randall, but it was a highly responsible Test innings and Randall will have to be prepared to play more like that one when the circumstances warrant if he is to fulfil his potential at Test level.

It was still a delicate position and I reckoned we must look for a lead of around 250. Then we could pressurise them with men round the bat to the spinners without regarding every slog for runs as a disaster. The rest day was a lull before another six hours of batting pressure.

Fourth day

They stuck up a poster on the Hill naming one of Packer's pylons as the Henry Blofly Stand – and after his articles in *The Australian* newspaper I'm not surprised he's popular among the yobs. Blofeld suggested in his match report that Brearley checked Randall in the middle of the pitch after he hooked a four, when in fact all Mike said was 'Good shot'! Amazing how omniscient a man can be sitting 120 yards away!

Brearley left the batsmen in no doubt that our aim was to see the whole day through. 'Go for your shots by all means but also imagine how we would feel in their position if we could not take a wicket early on,' he told Randall and Gooch. Runs would come more easily later on.

The heat was searing, England made a slow, deliberate start and a pattern developed which was to dominate the day: good shots, streaky shots, catches dropped and batsmen with plenty of patience. Had the catches been held, the whole complexion of the Test would have changed.

Randall was dropped after an hour, pushing forward to Higgs and offering a bat-pad chance to Border at gully. Fortunately for Randall the ball went to Border's weak right hand and he dropped it. Gooch had made 14 when he went down the pitch to drive Higgs and squeezed a straightforward catch to Hughes at second slip. Dropped again.

The new ball was due but Yallop didn't take it and I could see why. There was some turn in the pitch, Gooch was under pressure from four men round the bat and if Australia could get a wicket with the old ball they would still have the new one up their sleeve for the next batsman. On top of that, the pitch was getting slower and slower; the seamers were hard to hit using a soft old ball.

But Australia were frustrated and it showed on Yallop when Randall twice pulled away as Hurst began his run. A TV cameraman fell off the gantry above the sightscreen and there was a lot of commotion and movement to the side of the screen as Hurst came in, so Randall rightly pulled away. Yallop must have thought he was simply wasting time and he raced in from cover waving his arms about, telling Randall to get on with it. Quite a performance.

Gooch was out after battling on for 90 minutes. Wood dived and caught the ball at silly point as Gooch played forward to Higgs, but Gooch didn't walk, simply because he was not sure if the appeal was for a catch or lbw; he did not think he had touched it. 'Don't you think you're out when you're caught?' shouted a member as he walked in, and if looks could kill, NSW would be a subscription less. But Gooch was entitled to wait for the decision.

Gower got off to a flying start against Higgs bowling round the wicket, driving for threes, banging a full toss for four and sweeping for another four. Higgs switched to over the wicket and there was a big shout for a bat-pad catch to Wood at silly mid-on, then Gower drove hard and was almost caught and bowled.

Yallop finally took the new ball and, since Randall was in the nineties, Hogg tried to bounce him out. Randall hooked two in front of square for fours, waited until they put a man back for the shot and then hooked a third delicately down to fine leg for four more. Good thinking.

Hogg immediately employed the now familiar tactic of bowling round the wicket to Gower, who played away from his body towards cover off the back foot and was caught behind for 34. England 237-4.

And the Aussies still made life hard for themselves by dropping catches. Randall played back defensively and was dropped low at slip by Hughes off Higgs, and again when he was 117 he got an inside edge to a delivery from Hurst but Maclean dropped it two-handed behind the stumps. 'I'm ruddy well going to bat all day', said Randall at tea. He could, too.

Botham was tempted to hook by Hurst who had two men out for the shot, resisted some short-pitched deliveries and flirted dangerously with others. Perhaps he fancied his chances against Hurst because they played together in Melbourne. Believe it or not Randall was dropped – again – when a delivery from Higgs turned horrendously and he got an edge which flicked off the wicketkeeper's pads and was put down by Yallop at slip.

Fields were defensive and the bowling was searching, so

Botham resigned himself to a supporting role, not entirely through choice but admirably enough in view of our determination to bat all day. He had been in ninety minutes for six, amazing self-denial for him, when he played forward and too low to a delivery which took the shoulder of the bat and was caught by Wood at silly mid-off.

Randall's concentration was tremendous, especially considering he is a great talker at the crease. He talks to himself and is perfectly happy to have a chat with anybody within earshot, a habit which is not always appreciated and certainly not when he has scored a century and is still going strong. Hogg bowled a loose one. 'Too wide, mate, too wide,' said Randall – and Hogg informed him in lurid detail how straight the next one would be. When Yallop made a field change Randall chirped up helpfully: 'Wouldn't put him there, mate. Put him there, more use to you up there ...' Yallop did not seem to be too amused.

Miller was fortunate to survive an appeal for a bat-pad catch off Higgs; just as well because he still needed at least 75 runs for a negotiable lead. And Randall had a nasty moment on 149 when there was a big appeal for lbw, but he took a quick single to reach 150. It had taken him 9½ painstaking hours; a superb innings when the team needed one just like it and all the more praiseworthy because of his discipline.

He was out soon afterwards, lbw to a delivery bowled from wide of the crease by Hogg which hit his left leg in front of middle stump. The kind of ball which, delivered from wide of the crease, would be likely to miss leg stump – but we have noticed that umpires in Australia tend to uphold appeals if the ball hits the pad between wicket and wicket and to disregard angles.

Not long afterwards Bob Taylor, still in his crease, was hit by a half volley from Hogg which looked out from the pavilion. But the appeal was turned down and Hogg, not surprisingly, almost threw a fit.

We finished the day 162 ahead with four wickets in hand and regarded that as a fair achievement, even if Blofeld went on TV to say we should have batted more quickly. We would have liked to, but that involves a greater element of risk and we had already been lucky with dropped catches; we had not really insured ourselves against defeat so it was a bit premature to talk about lashing out to win.

There was a sequel to my first-ball dismissal which caused a brief stir. As I came off the field some guy made a provocative remark and I answered him tersely and to the point. Perhaps I should have stopped and shaken his hand, cracked a few jokes ... Anyway, one Australian newspaper carried a story saying this chap wanted a public apology; they only carried it for one edition and then it was taken out. And by the merest coincidence, the complainant turned out to be the same politician who had sent me (and the Press) a sarcastic telegram in Perth. He suggested we might shake hands publicly with a few photographers on hand to make sure it got in the papers. A really sincere offer, that.

Fifth day

There was a feeling of optimism in the dressing room. We were not entirely out of the wood but we felt we had a good chance of bowling them out, given a decent lead to bowl at. The most optimistic forecast was that we could get them out for 160, but that still meant we wanted quite a few more runs to enable us to put men round the bat to the spinners and not worry too much about the occasional boundary. We wanted runs in hand if we were to apply real pressure over a long period.

The pitch was slow, a dry turner on which a settled batsman could score runs given the right attitude and application. A very good Test pitch, which brought spinners into the game but enabled batsmen to play their shots; there ought to be more like it.

Miller was out lbw fairly early – again the feeling was that the delivery could have been missing leg stump – and Emburey suddenly found himself on the wrong end of a flurry of short-pitched balls from Hurst. He had been in for about half an hour, yet we were not allowed to bowl bouncers at Dymock earlier in the match when he had been in twice as long. We felt the inconsistency was infuriating. Embers mentioned it to the umpire but got no change because he was, it was considered, coping well enough.

The batsmen were told during drinks to keep playing sensibly; if the captain wanted them to accelerate he would signal from the pavilion. As it turned out, the signal would have been pointless; Emburey, trying to slog, sliced a catch to Darling at extra cover and Willis was caught at slip off his first ball. A few defiant shots from Hendrick and Taylor and the innings closed on 346. Australia needed 205 to win in four-and-a-half hours.

We felt we had done well to get back into the match after a dreadful first day; we might not win but we did not feel now that we were going to lose. I estimated they would face about sixty overs at most, which meant they would have to score at around three-and-a-half runs an over to win. Not too many Test sides manage that under pressure in the fourth innings, so they were going to have to bat really well.

Darling faced because Wood was on a pair, and the first ball from Willis whistled off the shoulder of the bat and might have been caught by an extra slip. Willis still looked dreadfully drained – he certainly wasn't fit – and David Gower had stayed in the hotel because of a sore throat. Willis had to leave the field after bowling only two overs, so a massive weight of responsibility fell on Hendrick to attack and contain from one end. He bowled superbly.

Emburey was struggling to find his rhythm and Wood swept and cut him for four. Then an almighty pull smacked into Botham's head at short square leg; if he had not been wearing a helmet I genuinely think it would have killed him. As it was, Botham tottered about groggily for quite a time, his head was ringing and he went into the outfield for a while. Gooch took over Botham's usual second slip spot against the seamer and took a very neat low catch when Darling got an edge. Australia 38–1 and the match about to change dramatically.

Wood played Miller to cover and set off. He really is the most appalling runner between the wickets: it's not a question of a communications breakdown, rather a matter of no communication at all. Hughes did not attempt to set off since Botham already had a hand on the ball; Wood made no atempt to change his mind, and both batsmen were standing at the bowler's end when Botham's throw reached Taylor above the stumps.

Suddenly they were under real pressure and we sensed they could not win. We did not feel under any pressure as a bowling side; the atmosphere on the field changed, we were on top. Yallop had only been in one over and already he was getting the slow handclap from a section of the crowd partly, one assumes, because of his repeated assertion that Australia would win and his claim that he always played the game in an attacking fashion. One or two of his verbal chickens had come home to roost.

Hendrick bowled a super line and length against him and then slipped in a slower ball. Yallop pushed through it and lobbed up a simple return catch; he stared quizzically at the pitch before walking away but I do not think the ball popped at all; I thought he misread the delivery.

Australia 45–3 and in more trouble than they could handle. On a slow, dry turner batsmen like Hughes and Toohey are relatively easy to bowl at because they are block, block, whack players who make very little attempt to knock the ball for ones and twos. 'Nurdling', we call it; Clive Radley is a past master. Hughes thumped Miller head-high and catchable just wide of Gooch at mid-off and hauled him over midwicket for four; down the wicket for big, booming drives and then block, block ... He is not going to get away with those tactics for long against Test class bowling.

Eventually Hughes played back defensively, was surprised when the ball turned, and popped a catch to short leg. Like so many Aussies batting against spin, he plays his strokes, even his defensive ones, too firmly. They do not wait for the ball and caress it with the spin.

Border was lucky to survive a delivery from Miller almost as soon as he came in, a bat-pad which Emburey just could not reach at silly mid-off, and Toohey sent one bat-pad off Emburey very fast to Botham's right. He could not hold it but the pressure took its toll. Toohey faced a 7–2 field to the off-spinners; he likes to drive on the off-side and he seemed to be trying to get inside the line of a fairly full, straight delivery when he was out. He yorked himself and Australia were 74–5.

There was just time for Maclean to win me $3 before tea. In view of his record against our spinners, Randall and I struck a bet: 'Three dollars says he doesn't last more than ten deliveries,' said Randall, so I took him on. The second ball from Miller became a huge, looping bat-pad which cleared Hendrick at short leg – much to Randall's chagrin – but in the last over before tea Miller went round the wicket and had him caught off his glove by Botham at silly point. It was the 11th ball he had faced.

The Test match was over. Australia were 76–6 and it was simply a matter of finishing them off – an amazing thought when you consider the state of the game at the start of play on that day. We were little over an hour from winning the Ashes again.

Dymock was promoted above Hogg, but he looked very shaky against Emburey, especially with five men round the bat. Emburey bowled him a slower ball just short of a length, Dymock tried to force it off the back foot and chopped it into his stumps; Australia 85–7. Hogg edged a bat-pad quickly but straight to Botham at short square leg: 85–8.

Border hung on defiantly. He looked a well-balanced and well-organised player, using a long stride down the pitch to smother the spin, driving and cutting Emburey for boundaries, pulling both offspinners over midwicket. But his latest partner was Higgs and I doubt if he had batted an hour all season! Still, he tried valiantly enough despite a cordon of seven men round the bat; we could not get a bat-pad and more accomplished batsmen than him had played plenty.

Emburey eventually went round the wicket and Higgs, misreading the length as so often happens when the angle of delivery is altered, played back and was lbw. He had faced 31 deliveries, a considerable feat for him, and the crowd gave him a good-natured ovation as he walked off.

Almost over, but not before a couple of false starts. Gooch took a catch at slip and we thought that was that, but the ball flicked Hurst's pad and not his bat. Then Brearley took a catch fielding very close on the on-side and hurled it jubilantly into the air; when it came down the appeal for a bat-pad was refused.

Border thumped Emburey miles into the air over mid-on and our substitute fielder John Lever whirled about trying to get under it. But it was a difficult chance, dropping over his shoulder as he ran round, and he did well to get a hand to it at all. After his drop, Lever confessed he kept thinking. 'Don't worry, Hurst can't possibly last an hour, can he? Can he ...?'

Hurst had a couple of slogs in an effort to force men away from the bat and finally edged a delivery from Emburey into his stumps. It was 5.05 pm on January 11th and England had retained the Ashes. The Ashes retained ... sounds like the title of a book to me.

What had gone wrong for Australia? I suspect they did not think carefully enough about what the situation demanded. The match was there for the winning and they seemed to think they could get away with a great deal of application or hard work; they did not work out the details of their approach. Test cricket is not simply about ability, it involves a willingness to think through situations, a good deal of tactical awareness. 'Let's get out there and win it,' is a fine cavalier attitude but it can have its pitfalls, as the Australians found out.

On the rest day of the Test, while most of the players were relaxing, Geoff Miller asked me if I would bat against him. We spent an hour in the middle at the Sydney ground with Miller bowling and bowling because, as he said: 'I might have to bowl to win this match.' That's the sort of attitude that wins Tests. I hate to say it because I have the greatest respect for Aussies as competitors – but they seem to have lost their understanding of what real Test cricket is all about. And I don't just mean the yobs who, whatever the sport and the occasion, are literally only there for the beer.

The Australian Press savaged their team after the Sydney defeat. They can help educate and mould public opinion, yet their response to events at Sydney was just a hatchet job, an hysterical outburst. Yallop was a hopeless captain, Australia were a rubbish team, the cricket was boring, etc, etc. It went on and on with practically no objective criticism or analysis of what had gone wrong.

Inevitably there was the parrot cry that Australia were no good without their Packer players, that this wasn't really the full Australia side and that the English, even using negative tactics, had won the series simply because they were playing a second eleven. Talk about whingeing Poms!

One newspaper immediately organised a poll to ask if readers thought Packer players should be reinstated (I wonder what the response would have been to the same question after our defeat at Melbourne) and there was a great deal of moaning and whining about individuals and the game in particular.

When they win everything is fine but when they lose they want an easy scapegoat and a quick remedy; but those things just aren't available in Test cricket. The Australian Press, public and informed element of the spectators should have been supporting and encouraging a young side in the knowledge that they would get better quicker with the backing of the public.

Aussies are great talkers; they love to lay the law down about everything under the sun and that's not an entirely un-attractive characteristic – it's part of their vitality and desire to be involved. But Test cricket takes time to learn, time to play and time to watch.

13 A sickening blow

Newcastle in Australia is very much like Scarborough in York-shire, a long bay sweeping away from the hotel round to a green headland. No castle on top, but still reminiscent of North Bay. A fine beach, too, but if we had any secret thoughts about time to enjoy it we were soon disillusioned.

Northern New South Wales made 223-9 declared, batting first on a good pitch. It seamed a bit on the first morning, turned slowly and lasted well through the three days of the match. They batted very well and we took the opportunity to give a long bowl to Lever, Old and Edmonds, who had not played in the last two Tests and were obviously short of match practice.

The reserve umpire at the match came up with an original thought. 'You know,' he confided, 'I never give anyone out lbw first ball. I have to get used to the light and the pitch and judge what the ball's doing first' – and naturally the lads advised him to have a chat with me!

When I got ready to bat through the last fifty minutes of the first day some joker had left me a message – written on my left pad. It said, 'Best wishes from Robin Bailhache' ... One of the umpires grinned: 'We aren't giving any lbws in this match, there have been far too many on the tour already.' It sounded like good news but as it turned out it didn't help me; I was caught down the leg side for 15, trying to glance.

The pitch turned slowly, quite unlike anything we had met on the tour so far, and I suspect several of the lads were unable to adjust themselves mentally to the change. We were bowled out for 163 by the NNSW spinners, Holland and Hill, and but for three determined innings we would have been in even greater trouble. Brearley batted really well for 66 and then Lever and Emburey spared a few blushes with a last-wicket stand which put on 50 in forty-one minutes. Even so, the country team had a lead of 60 runs.

The worst aspect of the innings was an injury to Roger Tolchard, our reserve wicketkeeper. He tried to hook the opening bowler Davis and was hit a sickening blow on the cheekbone; there was blood all over the place and we were really afraid that his eye might be damaged. Tolchard went to a local hospital and, mercifully, there was no eye damage, but the injury ruled him out of the rest of the tour and a stand-by wicketkeeper, David Bairstow, was called out from England. It was great to see David again and I'm glad he was called in, even though Warwickshire's Geoff Humpage was much closer at hand in Perth. David was desperately disappointed when he was not chosen to tour in the first place and to reject him as a replacement might have shattered his confidence and enthusiasm completely.

Gooch took over behind the stumps and did an admirable job, safe and competent if not (quite) as agile as Tolchard, but we had a devil of a job winkling the NNSW batsmen out. They sensed they might pull off a remarkable win and we had to permutate our bowlers and our tactics to get through them, sometimes spreading the field to tempt them and sometimes attacking with men round the bat. We took two wickets in the last ten minutes, otherwise it would have looked really gloomy from our point of view.

At the start of the third day NNSW were looking for a lead of 280 and a run-a-minute challenge which would have given them a real chance of winning. It never materialised because Edmonds took a wicket with his first ball and Old ran through the tail. We had four hours and forty minutes to make 227 to win.

I was still troubled by soreness in my left knee. I had slipped getting out of a car in Sydney and some of the old trouble flared up; a doctor in Newcastle confirmed there was muscle wastage and recommended treatment and exercises to build it up.

Brearley and I put on a century for the first wicket; nothing dramatic, just playing sensibly and taking runs where they became available. And after Brearley was out, caught at backward short leg trying to lift the offspinner over midwicket, Radley and I carried on in much the same fashion. It was considered and professional, too professional for the NNSW bowlers, well as they played.

A victory was no more than was expected of us, but the captain pointed out that even this match had highlighted an annoying habit we had developed. We batted poorly in the first innings and had to work really hard in the second innings to redeem ourselves.

Brearley took a rest when we moved on to Tasmania and he deserved one. Every captain on a long tour needs some time away from the team and the media, because the responsibilities on and off the field are so onerous these days.

14 Our separate ways

Tasmania is probably the most English of the Australian states: green and rolling, dominated by the tree-covered hump of Mt Wellington and the beautiful Derwent river estuary spanned by the impressive Tasman bridge. The weather is pretty English, too, if only because you can't rely on it.

Shortly before we arrived in Launceston, Tasmania beat Western Australia in the Gillette Cup final, thanks largely to a superb all-round performance from their captain, Lancashire's Jack Simmons.

Naturally they were over the moon and we were sure of a big crowd at the one-day match in Launceston; it was Tasmania's first trophy and the win fired everybody with confidence and enthusiasm. The ground was small but well appointed and nicely situated among trees; by the start of the match it was groaning at the seams with spectators.

We opened with Miller after winning the toss, but he was out to the first ball he received; Radley and I got out after seeing off the new ball. Then Randall, Gower, Botham and Edmonds went to town, the ball kept disappearing into the trees and although the crowd loved it, I don't think the Tasmanian bowlers were too impressed.

After we made 240–8 it was barely a contest. The Tasmanian batsmen had little idea against a class bowling attack on a pitch which did a bit, Edmonds bowled extremely well and they were all out 77. It was a sobering experience after their heady Gillette Cup victory and Flat Jack told them a few home truths after the match; if they were going to press for full Sheffield Shield status, this was hardly the way to go about it.

The three-day match, played at Hobart in a beautiful setting with the estuary on one side and the mountains on the other, was bedevilled by the weather. On the second day mist and rain began to creep down from the mountains like thick white smoke, and only eighty-five minutes of cricket were possible before play was washed out for the day.

We won the toss, put them in on a pitch which bounced unevenly and helped the seamers, and soon had them in all kinds of trouble. Old bowled beautifully for 2¾ hours and finished with six for 42, but in so doing he aggravated strained stomach muscles and did his long-term tour prospects no good at all. It was a great pity he should bowl so well and come out of it with another injury problem.

They were all out for 105 – it might have been considerably less if we had taken all our catches or they had connected with every ball they played at – and we made 101–3 to the close. I was 41 and much happier with myself; I felt a lot more comfortable than I had for some time.

The pitch was supposed to have been cut, but it looked even greener next morning and we struggled for runs before the rain came.

When the match was washed out I went with Bob Taylor and Bernie Thomas to play Royal Tennis. It's a fascinating game quite unlike lawn tennis and I confess I'm still not sure of all the rules and practices, but I played quite a bit at Melbourne in 1971 when the Test was completely washed out – Colin Cowdrey introduced me to it – and I know it well enough to get by.

The rain had been pretty steady all day and late into the evening and the start of the third day was delayed until 1.00 pm. We decided to bat on and eventually declared with a lead of 105. Geoff Miller batted very well and I was so-so; the ball was still seaming about and it was not easy to pierce defensive fields. I kept striking the ball hard and sweetly but straight to fielders; very frustrating.

We had three hours to bowl them out and we made a determined bid with our seamers at the start. But Old had to go off because of stomach trouble after bowling only five overs, so we decided to give the spinners some match bowling practice. Tassy batted through for a draw, helped by a competent 46 not out from John Hampshire.

There were a couple of unusual incidents during the match, but I suppose everyone was waiting to see how Hampshire and I would react in our first meeting since he was made captain of Yorkshire. Kerry Packer wrote a letter to Mike Brearley offering to play an Australian Packer team against England for a 50,000-dollar prize, an obvious publicity stunt which was inevitably turned down. Then David Bairstow went to hospital with a suspected broken nose after one of the most bizarre injuries I can recall; he was doing strengthening exercises with Bernie Thomas when a hand slipped, a grip was lost and Bernie's backside crashed down into Bairstow's face! Blood rushed into David's mouth, he could hardly breathe and they nipped him off to hospital in case his nose was broken. David's nose being what it is, it's not easy to tell when it's straight and when it's bent. Fortunately there was no break but it looked pretty sore and his left eye was black for a couple of days.

Then there was Hampshire. He was quoted as having told an English newspaper he was ready to try to sort things out between us, but in fact he made no effort to do so. 'I intend to try and make things up between us. I can't see any reason why I shouldn't – we have known and played alongside each other for twenty years and there's never been any trouble before. I have no animosity towards Geoff and if he wants to make it difficult between us, that's up to him,' said Hampshire.

I did not see that it was my duty to go to him. After all, he was the new Yorkshire captain with a responsibility to all his players and, let's face it, after the Northants business there was no doubt who was the injured party between us. I was let down by him, not the other way round, and if he had any grievances it was up to him as a senior player to voice them to me. He never said a word; he just went out and made his personal feelings known at the cost of Yorkshire's reputation. At no time did Hampshire make a genuine effort to speak to me, unless he regards a cursory three-word remark as he was going to bat as a conversation. The Press soon spotted that there was little contact between us and of course it made stories back home. I still insist that in view of his conduct at North-ampton, it was up to Hampshire to make a conciliatory gesture to me. As it was, we went our separate ways. He was out for a duck in the first innings, edging a half volley from Old to Taylor, and made a steady 46 not out in the second.

15   Lifesaver Emburey

Rodney Hogg had not bowled himself into the record books –
not quite – when he made an assessment which was to be
proved positively clairvoyant during an extraordinary first
day in Adelaide. Hogg said the pitch wasn't ready for use as
a Test pitch and needed another day and a half to dry out.
Gypsy Petulengro strikes again . . .

   The pitch was firm with a good covering of grass. It had
been well rolled and it was clear it would seam for a while and
probably turn on the fourth or fifth day; not an easy decision
for the side winning the toss. On balance I think we would
have opted to bat – and as it turned out we had no choice because Yallop won the toss and put us in.

   That was something of a surprise, but I reckon it was a
decision taken partly out of determination and partly out of a
spirit of self-preservation. Hogg was keen to bowl on it, so
Yallop naturally asked himself what Willis and Hendrick
might do to his batsmen if he decided to bat first. But his
decision meant that Australia would have to bat last on a pitch
which traditionally tends to turn, and our spinners had made
pretty short work of them in Sydney. A difficult situation.

   It looked as though his gamble had paid off handsomely
inside the first hour when we were 27 for 5 and the Aussie
crowd were crowing their side to victory. Thanks to Botham
and Miller we reached 169; then it was Australia's turn to
struggle – 69–4 at the close and a long way from being on top
in the match. Quite a day.

   The first five wickets went down like ninepins. Hogg
bowled quick, naturally keen to impress his home crowd, and
Hurst is always an awkward customer, difficult to judge for
length because his body is well round in the delivery stride and
the ball is hidden until it is released with a slinging action.

He bowled one which left me a bit and Kevin Wright took his first catch behind the stumps.

Brearley appeared unlucky, given out caught behind off a delivery from Hogg which bounced appreciably; he clearly thought it had brushed his upper arm and not his bat or glove. But the decision stood.

Gooch went next, ducking late into a short, quick delivery from Hogg which hit his glove and leaped via his helmet in a gentle arc to Hughes at slip, and then Randall fell to a magnificent catch.

He was probably over-confident, having survived a big appeal for lbw off Hurst, and tried to drive a wide delivery square on the off-side. It slid off the face of the bat and Carlson dived wide at fourth slip to take a great catch when the ball seemed to be almost past him.

Hogg went round the wicket to Gower – that ploy again – but it was Hurst who dismissed him, cramping him for room with a delivery which ducked into him and trapped him lbw half forward. England 27–5 ... and the match had to pause for drinks!

Botham and Miller had a heavy responsibility and they carried it with real determination. They gritted it through to lunch at a time when it was absolutely imperative we did not lose another wicket – not exactly in command but obviously aware of their responsibilities. Miller looked sketchy: he played and missed a lot, nicked a couple of boundaries through and wide of slip and should really have been out before he scored but Hurst misjudged the flight at fine leg and barely got a hand to the ball when he hooked at Carlson. Yardley replaced Hurst shortly before lunch but I would have given Higgs a go; Botham had not batted particularly well against him; but he played very well; a disciplined, controlled innings to help take the score to 71–5 at lunch.

Miller was out soon after the restart, having batted eighty invaluable minutes for 31. He was beaten by Hogg's nip-back ball – not the first man to suffer that fate on this tour – though there was some suggestion that the ball might have been going down.

Taylor was dropped by Border at second slip off Hogg and

Botham suddenly showed the more familiar, more aggressive side of his nature when Yardley came on for Carlson. Botham whacked him over midwicket for six, over mid-on for an all-run four and then cut him for three in the same over. He was going so well that Taylor recognised the need to protect him – and that led to an unnecessary run-out.

When Yardley went round the wicket Botham swept him and embarked on an all-run four as Hogg chased at fine leg. As he set off for the fourth Botham slipped and Taylor, anxious in case Botham could not make it to the danger end, tried to send him back. But Both kept going and got in; Taylor was late setting off and Wright had time to underarm Hogg's return for the bowler to run Taylor out. He had scored only four himself but he had supported Botham for almost an hour.

Botham was getting into his stride and Australia put mid-on back and posted a man deep at midwicket. He had a life when he swept Yardley and Hogg dropped an easy catch; Hurst suffered for that when he was hooked over fine leg for four and smacked off the back foot head-high through square cover for four next ball.

Higgs replaced Yardley and Emburey fell to a poor shot, playing across the line. Both tried to get after Higgs – he has not played him with much confidence – and he was finally caught at the wicket trying to drive. Wright took the bails off for good measure and Botham was so far forward he would have been given out either way. As their paths crossed, Botham advised Willis to play his shots rather than poke about with men in catching positions. And that led to an extraordinary twenty-five minutes.

I don't suppose many of Willis's shots will end up in the MCC coaching manual – not unless a giant, spidery swipe at the ball becomes one of cricket's legitimate strokes of the future. But runs are runs and Willis contributed 24; who was going to carp about the way he got them? He plonked his left foot to leg and whacked Hurst over cover for six, slogged the next ball for two over mid-on. Another slog over the slips (cunning, that) for four, then a great swipe over extra cover for four. Willis gave himself plenty of room outside the leg stump and Hurst tried to counteract that by chasing him with the ball; they both ended up twelve inches outside the leg stump at one stage; I wasn't too sure which pitch they were playing on.

The crowd chanted for the return of Hogg, and he duly replaced a rather perplexed Hurst, spread his field and bowled a slow offspinner which Willis promptly banged for four; but it couldn't last and Willis finally sent the ball into orbit with a mighty heave, Darling looked as though he had misjudged it but pulled off a very good catch and we were all out 169. It had taken Australia three and three-quarter hours to do it, and Yallop must have been well satisfied with his decision to put us in.

It was a difficult position for us but it might not be a desperate one if we attacked them and gave absolutely nothing away. So we started with the ever-reliable Hendrick rather than Botham, who can be rather more expensive.

Willis's first over produced a near-tragic sensation. He cut back a delivery which hit Darling under the heart, the batsman collapsed in terrible trouble and our lads gesticulated frantically for some sort of help. Emburey gave Darling a thump in the chest which got him breathing with a gasp but his tongue was stuck in the back of his mouth and a wad of chewing gum was helping to block his breathing. Australia's physiotherapist finally got Darling on to his side and freed his breathing, but he was still only semi-conscious when he was stretchered off. They used oxygen to revive him on the way to hospital and he recovered quickly enough to come back to the ground, but it might have been very much worse.

Australia were soon in trouble of a different kind. Hughes became apprehensive when a delivery from Hendrick nipped back sharply as he played forward; he played at the next delivery tentatively and Emburey fell forward at gully to take a bat-pad catch.

Yallop was deceived by Hendrick too. He shaped to play at a delivery, then looked to leave it and was dumbfounded when it seamed into him and bowled him off a fine inside edge and pad. Australia 10-2.

Botham replaced Willis but Border looked in good form, playing his shots confidently. He clipped Botham for two off his legs and square cut him for four, so Botham gave him a couple of bouncers to force him on to the back foot. When he pitched one up, Border drove and edged it to Taylor; a typical example of a quick bowler outsmarting a batsman.

Yardley likes to whack the ball if the pitch is doing a bit, so Brearley spread the field even to having a man on the boundary behind point and another at fine third man behind the slips for the top edge. Sure enough, Yardley top-edged his first delivery from Botham over the slips for four. Willis came back but he was top-edged for four and driven through cover superbly for another boundary; he was struggling to find his rhythm, annoyed with himself for being able to muster little above medium pace.

While all the fur and feathers were flying Wood plugged away, batting sensibly and steadily, though he obviously found runs hard to come by. He played and missed occasionally, but the ball hit the middle of the bat more often than not. Willis went round the wicket and bowled wide of the off stump to neutralise Wood's favourite on-side shots, and he became frustrated enough to drive at a widish delivery but Botham put the chance down at second slip.

Hendrick replaced Willis just before the close and Yardley offered a low catch, again to Botham – and he dropped it. It's unusual for Botham to drop catches but he said he didn't really see that one; he looked as though he had come up too early and had to go down again to try and take the catch.

Australia finished the day on 69–4 – fourteen wickets in the day and great entertainment for the crowd; I would be the last person to underestimate the value of that. But I cannot genuinely believe you have a proper Test match surface when so many wickets go down on the first day. Come to think of it, throughout the series so far we had not come across a pitch where a captain winning the toss could be absolutely sure that he would bat first.

The ground was filled with just over 25,000 spectators, so it was a great atmosphere. Many of them disappeared after tea, but that is customary in Adelaide when local TV shows the last session and lots of spectators head for home to beat the traffic and get out of the hot sun.

Second day

It was imperative to attack Wood and Yardley from the outset
and Botham at his best was the man for that, especially since
Willis was struggling so desperately for form. Botham himself
wasn't bowling as well as we knew he could so we stirred him
up in the dressing room – and the result was amazing. It was
the old, belligerent Botham steaming in uphill, hostile and
aggressive. There is no doubting that Botham in this mood is
every inch a Test player; he was positively intimidating.

Yardley went quickly. He shaped to play his square slash
and the ball came back, flicked off his glove and hit the underside of his right arm before breaking the wicket. Australia
72–5.

Darling resumed his innings – chest well protected this
time. Both he and Wood like to hook and Botham is always
ready to hand out a challenge. Wood was disciplined enough
not to accept it but Darling is Darling, the compulsive if not
always happy hooker. Botham put two men on the fence to
underline the challenge, Darling cleared them once for six
and then hammered the ball down Bob Willis's throat, a pretty
predictable end.

If Botham is going to bowl bouncers – and he always will –
he should bowl them like this; quick and hostile while he is
fresh and the batsmen are relatively new. There's not a lot of
point in loosing bouncers when he is tired, batsmen are set
and the ball is a fortnight old.

Wood played steadily and responsibly, using his feet well
and showing good judgement. Emburey replaced Botham and
brought Randall squarer near the boundary, because he felt
sure Wood was going to sweep him off the stumps – and not
long afterwards Wood swept straight into Randall's hands. At
least Randall made it look easy; it fell just short of him but he
simply stooped forward and picked it up as though it was the
easiest catch in the world.

The injury to Darling had obviously had an effect on
Hogg. He is not the happiest batsman against fast bowling
and to his white helmet he now added a couple of yards of
chest protection. He could probably have survived a rifle bullet
at twenty-two yards. Unfortunately his first delivery from

Willis was a straight one and he missed it : Australia 116–8.

Wright impressed me a lot on his Test debut. He had kept wicket very well and now he batted well and thoughtfully, careful, yet prepared to play a shot under pressure. We reckoned he was caught behind when he had scored two; there appeared to be a big inside deflection and Taylor took the ball diving a long way to his left, but Wright got the benefit of the doubt. He batted for seventy-six minutes and made a valuable 29 before Emburey went on for Willis just before lunch and Wright was lbw working across a straight delivery.

We were looking for a lead of about 25 but Hurst and Higgs clung on; they were prepared to ride their luck and why not? There wasn't much hope of them making many if they pushed and prodded. They made 31 together; very frustrating for us but I could not see what else we might have done to separate them. Higgs eventually picked the wrong man when he attempted a sharp single to Gower at cover; it really is amazing how often he hits the wickets.

Perhaps we were hypercritical of ourselves but we felt genuinely disappointed not to have finished the innings with a lead of 20 or so instead of five. After being 27–5 it was a great fight-back to bowl out Australia for 164 and have a lead at all.

Suddenly, it was a one-innings pressure match to be played over 3½ days, a real test of application and attitude. Australia had lost the advantage of winning the toss; they would have to pick it up somewhere else because we had stayed with them and they had to bat last. But it was still a fraught situation.

Australia sensed the dangers and the possibilities every bit as forcefully as we did. Hogg raced in as though he meant it and Hurst – so often unsung but a superb bowler on this tour – was as quick and aggressive as anything we had faced. Carlson seams and swings the ball like an English bowler and mixes his deliveries imaginatively; we weren't going to be given any favours and it was important we made a good start.

Hogg retired from the firing line without taking a wicket, which has not happened too often. We put on 31 before Brearley was out. He probably should have been a little further forward when a delivery from Carlson cut back and kept low.

Randall played sensibly for almost an hour until he got involved in an exchange of the verbals with Hurst and determined to take him on. Hurst put an extra man in the midwicket area for the hook but Randall insisted on having a go – and Yardley took a fine catch, shielding his eyes as the ball swirled up into the sun but judging his position perfectly. I thought Randall should have disciplined himself better in the circumstances.

Australia switched their bowlers, Gooch battled through a difficult early spell when he didn't seem to pick the ball up too well, and we were 82–2 at the close with a lead of 87.

I had batted 189 minutes for 38 under pressure all the time but feeling quite confident, moving my feet better than I had for weeks. The desire to score runs is always there in that situation but so is the knowledge that you simply must not lose wickets. You always feel slightly apprehensive, reluctant to chance your arm against anything but an obviously loose ball.

I thought: if we can get 300 we should win the Test; if we get 250 we have a good chance. But the pitch is getting better and Australia have come at us hard. They are keeping the pressure on because they know they can still win the match.

There was a sombre footnote to Darling's injury. Our physiotherapist Bernard Thomas advised us all against chewing gum at the wicket, chiefly because it could become jammed in the windpipe if the kiss of life was necessary. It was a macabre thought, but the sight of a player like Darling grovelling in the crease makes you think about things like that.

Third day
We knew the first session might be a vital one. It was a hot day and their opening attack could struggle if they didn't make a breakthrough early on; we didn't expect to score easily but we had to grit it out. It didn't quite work out that way ...

Carlson moved the ball about a bit and bowled several wide deliveries – then got Gooch out with a straight ball! He played down the wrong line and the ball bowled him through a gap between bat and pad. England 97–3 and a shock we could have done without.

Hogg decided he had to go off. He complained of a tightening of the muscles in his thigh and insisted he couldn't carry on, though Yallop did his best to persuade him otherwise. I don't know what the cricket definition of mutiny is but Hogg must have come pretty close; they exchanged a few words then Hogg ignored Yallop and strode off. Yallop chased off the field later to see how Hogg was faring because he wanted him back to take the new ball; it was an undignified situation for a captain of Australia, to say the least.

Hurst bowled his heart out, quick and competitive, full of devil although the temperature was over 100 degrees and he had to bowl a long spell – twelve overs on the trot either side of lunch. He let me have two nasty bouncers and I weaved inside the first at shoulder height and ducked the second; this was no situation for anything as risky as hooking. We weren't exactly creaming the ball about and perhaps I became a little anxious to push the score along; I tried to slide a delivery through gully, it bounced and Hughes took a good catch head-high at first slip.

Botham and Gower had a lot to do and I suspected that Botham wouldn't last too long. Not because he was struggling but on the contrary because he looked too free and frisky. He smacked Hurst hard on the up to mid-off and thumped him off the back foot to cover, strong aggressive strokes which showed the mood Botham was in. Hurst outsmarted him. He slipped in a slower ball and Botham, into his stroke too soon, spotted the danger and tried to adjust his shot. All he got was a thick edge and Yardley took the catch comfortably at third slip.

Five minutes later we were in even deeper trouble. Higgs came on for Carlson and Gower drove him for four off the back foot and pulled him for two. But Higgs went round the wicket – every bowler uses that tactic against Gower now – and the ball pitching outside the off stump spun into him a bit. Gower tried to pull a delivery which was not all that short and missed. The ball would have hit middle stump if his pad had not been in the way.

A bad morning for England – 50 runs and four wickets. We were in a lot of trouble and the Test match seemed to have swung, perhaps decisively, in Australia's favour.

Miller and Taylor had other thoughts. Miller hooked Hurst for two fours, Taylor belted a full toss from Higgs for four and straight drove him stylishly for three. The new ball was taken but Yallop persevered with Carlson and Hurst before putting on Hogg; it was noticeable that when Hogg was brought back earlier he bowled only a couple of half-hearted overs and was then taken off.

By the time Hogg got his hands on the new ball Hurst had bowled a magnificent spell, an hour before lunch and fifty-five minutes after. He had done as much as he could possibly do to break the stand; another wicket at that stage really would have been the beginning of the end as far as we were concerned.

Taylor played really well. He got well forward to the seamers, more so than at any time on tour, and was ready to work the ball off his legs or accept a thick edge wide of gully for runs. They all count and Bob looked in super form, playing Yardley particularly well, pushing, glancing and off-driving confidently. Miller was perhaps a little more subdued but he drove Carlson for three and kept the score moving.

They put on 50 in seventy minutes and went sailing on after tea, Taylor passing his previous best Test score of 45 and the score mounting steadily as Australia fumed with frustration. Taylor on-drove Yardley for four and pushed Higgs for a single to bring up the century partnership. Miller looked as though he might be fretting a bit when he lifted Yardley over midwicket for four, but his 50 came up soon afterwards with a leg glance for three off Yardley again.

When the partnership reached 118 it became the best-ever for England's seventh wicket in an Adelaide Test, beating the previous best by Hobbs and Hendren during the 1924–5 tour. I wonder if their stand was as vital as this one?

Taylor was dropped by Border at slip off Higgs, a very difficult chance low to his left hand, and when Hurst came back into the firing line Yallop put the pressure on Taylor with slips, a gully and men close to the bat square on both sides of the wicket. Taylor promptly on-drove Hurst for an all-run four and short square leg was taken out to mid-on.

Hurst finally broke the partnership when Miller tried to leg glance and was caught behind by the diving Wright. Umpire Bailhache waited for the nod from square leg that the ball had carried before raising his finger; it seemed to take him half an hour. The stand had lasted 231 minutes and put on 135 priceless runs: Miller had batted five minutes longer than that for 64. A magnificent innings in pressure circumstances.

Australia's fields had become pretty defensive as Miller and Taylor forged on; now they pressured Emburey with five men round the bat and Border tested Taylor with chinamen and four fielders round the bat. Taylor survived an appeal for a stumping and when Border reverted to orthodox spin he drove him off the back foot through cover for four. When a single was available Taylor refused it, in order to protect Emburey from the strike until the last ball of the over.

We finished the day 272-7, a remarkable performance when you consider we were almost down and out at lunch. Bob Taylor was 69 not out after batting for 4½ hours – a superb achievement which might yet win us the match. But there was a snag – Botham had strained a thigh muscle ducking under a bouncer from Hurst and we were obviously going to need him fully fit if we were to bowl Australia out.

Fourth day
Taylor and Emburey had a double responsibility when play started with England 272-7. Naturally we wanted to press on and get as many runs as possible but in that heat – well into the nineties and beyond – we also did not want to have to bowl more than two sessions. So they had to create a balance between getting on with it and making sure they did not get out.

And they did it remarkably well. I have never seen Bob Taylor play better, especially against Hurst, who was Australia's best bowler; both batsmen got on to the front foot whenever they could and runs came without the need to slog or take unnecessary risks.

Hogg was at the ground early, having a fitness test to see how he would go in the rest of the match. The Press had been full of stories about so-called clashes between him and Yallop but he was in a cheerful enough mood. 'You're a damned nuisance,' I said. 'You're in the papers every day because you keep taking wickets and the first day you don't get a wicket at all you're still on the front page. I wish you'd behave yourself.' He grinned and muttered something I couldn't hear; perhaps just as well.

Carlson and Hurst bowled for forty minutes, Hurst apparently saving himself for the new ball which wasn't far away. Taylor drove him straight a couple of times while Emburey played carefully and mainly on the defensive – until Yardley came on. Then Emburey had a rush of blood; over midwicket for four, through mid-off for four next ball and then a drop at slip by Border.

Runs came steadily against Higgs and Yardley, a push here and a boundary there, and Hogg finally replaced Higgs at 322–7 with the new ball due. He and Hurst ran in really trying, and poor Taylor got out for 97, three short of a century which he so richly deserved. He tried to leg glance and was caught behind by Wright diving to his left – and disappointed or not, Taylor walked immediately. He had batted for over six hours when England needed an innings of character and quality and shown plenty of both; a marvellous performance.

Emburey chipped Hogg for two and pulled him for four, all useful runs well made, until he missed a half volley from Hogg and was bowled. And Williis gave a brief exhibition of his own particular style of batsmanship before slogging hugely and edging a catch to the wicketkeeper. England 360; Australia needed 366 to win in about 9½ hours.

It was a formidable total, more than I expected we would need as the match developed, but Brearley had some sound advice before they went in. 'Let's not go out there thinking we have enough and wickets will fall eventually. Let's see if we can bowl them out for 200.' It was an ambitious thought but at least it gave us a target and guarded against complacency; a shrewd thought on the captain's part.

Willis had been struggling for some time to find rhythm and confidence. He set off from one mark and four deliveries later found himself three yards away from it; a desperate plight for any quick bowler. He immediately went round the wicket to neutralise Wood's favourite leg-side shots and he tried desperately hard, but the flow simply wasn't there. Australia battted sensibly and well until Botham came on.

Darling has a habit of shuffling across in order to work the ball on the leg side. English players would probably let it come into their body but Darling likes to get right over, which makes his leg stump an inviting target. Darling left it unprotected and Botham, never one to miss an opportunity, promptly knocked it out.

Hughes came in and got off the mark with five runs, which doesn't happen every day. He thick-edged Botham for three and Gooch's throw cleared Taylor by a mile, so they ran two overthrows. That brought Wood down to the striker's end and he seemed very fortunate to survive an appeal for caught behind down the leg-side off Botham.

Before the innings started I had told Derek Randall I intended running somebody out and he reacted with a rather predictable snort of disbelief. I suppose if I had been asked to nominate the lucky player I would have chosen Wood, if only on the balance of probability. Wood played steadily, not scoring runs very quickly but looking sound and composed – until he pushed a delivery from Botham towards me at mid-on and kept on going. I suppose I was fifteen yards away from the wicket and I had only one stump to aim at, so I took a little bit of time to measure the throw. And Wood was still a yard out when the wicket was broken.

Wood complained to umpire Bailhache that Botham had impeded him, and since Botham was bowling round the wicket at the time there may be something in that; Wood certainly had to make a bit of a detour. But there was no suggestion that Botham intended to impede the batsman and in any case it's up to a batsman to avoid a fielder and not the other way round. The umpires were in a good position to see what happened and they had no doubts about the legality of the dismissal.

Yallop was on a pair and we made sure he stayed nervous and runless for as long as possible, then Miller kept him guessing by pitching into the bowlers' footmarks just outside the line of the stump. Miller and later Emburey persuaded the odd delivery to turn slowly, Botham tried to tempt Hughes to hook without much success and the batsmen seemed to be going quite steadily.

Then they slowed down to a virtual standstill. It was difficult to see why but Yallop became completely becalmed and Hughes, despite his ability to get down the wicket and play a superbly straight bat, seemed totally unable to knock off ones and twos.

There was no screaming urgency in their situation but their inactivity left Aussie a bit short at the end of the day – 82 for 2, still needing 284 to win the match. I got the impression that they did not really know whether they were trying to win the match or save it; had they already conceded that the target was too big, especially since two wickets had gone, or were they determined to have a go? If they were going to win they would have to bat far better in the fourth innings than either side on the tour so far, but if they decided to save it they had a good chance provided they batted responsibly. They had a much better chance of saving it than winning it, but they would have to decide that for themselves – and pretty early next morning.

Fifth day
It looked as though they had decided to go for the win. Yallop and Hughes started very well, aggressive and enterprising without taking too many risks, and put on twenty-four runs in the first twenty minutes. Yallop lifted Emburey over midwicket for four and drove him off the back foot through the covers for three; Hughes coverdrove Miller superbly.

Brearley said he would give the spinners a go early on, but bring on the seamers if a wicket did not go quickly: Yallop is far happier against spin than seam. The rate at which Australia were going helped force his hand and Hendrick and Botham soon replaced the offspinners.

Yallop doesn't fancy Hendrick one bit. He is anxious against him and leaves quite a few deliveries, never quite sure where his off stump is or what Hendrick will do with the ball. When he had made 36 he studiously left a delivery from Hendrick which pitched just outside off stump – and it did enough to bowl him.

Hughes tried to drive a delivery rather too short for the shot and the ball squirmed fast and low off the bat to point, where Gower took an acrobatic catch as he rolled over. And incredible as it now seems, they were finished: The Test match was won and lost. Australia had lost four wickets for 120 and, so it seemed, all their stomach for a long, hard fight. They crumpled hopelessly to 160 all out.

Border was tied down for thirty-one minutes for a single before Willis replaced Hendrick. It was another hot day and it made sense not to bowl the quicker bowlers in long spells with the new ball not far away. And Willis's first ball was a beauty. He went round the wicket to the left-hander, drew him forward and moved the ball between bat and pad from outside the off stump to bowl him. It was a superb length delivery for the first ball of a spell, especially since Willis had been struggling so hard to find his rhythm and confidence.

Perhaps the dismissal of Yardley summed up better than any other the sort of problem which cost Australia so dear. Yardley blocked the first ball and then launched into his famous all-or-nothing front-foot drive – and was caught by Brearley at first slip. What on earth was any Australian batsman doing playing a shot like that to the second delivery he faced with a Test match already slipping away fast? He should have been fighting to save it, setting out his stall for a really long and disciplined innings, not trying to slog the ball out of sight. Lack of orders? Lack of self-discipline? Whatever the root cause I thought it was very irresponsible. A double wicket maiden for Willis and Australia had just lost four wickets for six runs!

Carlson was on a pair in his first Test match and Botham and Hendrick gave him a nerve-racking time before he drove Botham through cover and galloped for three with a big sigh of relief. His patience must have been all but exhausted.

Wright had distinguished himself in the first innings but there was to be no repetition of that. He was put under pressure with men close to the bat on both sides of the wicket and Willis steaming in. Not the Willis who struggled so badly in the first innings but the one who started the tour full of optimism and enthusiasm. The ball whistled through – and the old ball at that – all the old Willis rhythm was back and Wright must have thought it was a different game altogether. Playing and missing and fending the ball off ribs and chest isn't anybody's idea of fun cricket but Wright stuck it out for nearly twenty minutes until Miller came back into the attack. Four men perched round the bat and Wright was caught off bat and pad on the leg side.

It seemed ages before Hogg emerged but he finally hauled himself to the wicket for a brief stay. He clipped Miller for two over midwicket but then played a very lazy stroke to a delivery which turned a little – and was bowled off stump. At lunch Australia were 131–8; I don't know if they ate a hearty meal. They had lost six wickets for forty-nine runs in the morning, six for fifteen in one horrendous hour. Perhaps they ate humble pie ...

The end wasn't delayed for long. Carlson played some enterprising shots – through the covers off Willis, a four off the back foot against Miller – before Hendrick took the new ball. Then he tried to drive on the up, a poor shot in the circumstances, and Gower took another good catch at square leg. Hurst had a couple of magic moments with nothing to lose by attacking until Willis yorked him leg stump. It was just after 2.00 pm and Australia's ambitions of winning the match or batting all day to save it had collapsed in ruins.

The Australian Press gave their side a real roasting, as they invariably do in these circumstances, and to be honest there was little enough that the Aussies could be proud of in their performance. I thought Bobby Simpson summed it up best. 'While the England bowlers were bowling a good line and length, the dismissals had to be put down to gross indiscretions on the part of the batsmen,' said Simpson. 'The odd lapse is acceptable but not the inconsistency shown in this series.

'The only answer is that they are not applying themselves sufficiently to the demands of Test cricket and don't seem desperate enough to succeed.'

I still find it hard to believe that they could be bowled out for that score on that pitch. It was easily the best fourth- and fifth-day pitch we had met in the series and we should have been made to work, sweat and suffer by every batsman from one to eleven. In fact we took three wickets and the rest gave it away.

It is easy to blame Yallop, but he cannot bat, bowl and field for everyone. The public want a scapegoat when things go wrong and the captain is fair game, but it's often a superficial point of view. Australia's bowlers have not let them down – England had hardly made big scores throughout the series – but their batsmen had failed time and time again.

What's basically wrong? The biggest difference between the sides is experience and professionalism; I have made that point before and no doubt I'll make it again. And to help bridge the gap I would give them a team manager with a deep knowledge of the game and the ability to tell individual players where they are going wrong and how they might put things right. A man to whom the players could listen with respect because he had proved his ability at the highest level. And the obvious candidate for the job is Bob Simpson.

We left Adelaide in high spirits. Our victory meant we did not face the possibility of a six-day Test in Sydney which we didn't believe in anyway, and our performance again had been impressive. We don't have one star who does all the work; every player is capable of chipping in with a vitally important contribution and the fifth Test underlined that fact very clearly. A fascinating match before a big crowd – and the best behaved crowd in Australia at that. It was a good feeling.

16 Slipping and sliding

I suppose Tasmania were the last team we expected to meet in Melbourne on February 3rd, but Jack Simmons inspired them to a marvellous victory in the Gillette Cup final and they were naturally anxious to impress their claim for full Sheffield Shield status with a good performance against the tourists.

Unfortunately, the match was a bit of a farce. For a start the square at the MCG was in a terrible condition. There were huge areas of black soil all over the square and especially at the pavilion end, patches of grass here and there. It looked like the remains of an opencast pit near Barnsley.

Then there was the weather. It is notoriously unpredictable in Victoria – the locals have a saying: If you don't like our weather, just wait a minute – and the sky was slate-grey and overcast. A local weather station insisted it wouldn't rain but we reckoned we knew better from where we were standing.

I couldn't help reflecting that it was in this match eight years ago – against the then Gillette Cup winners Western Australia – that my arm was broken by a delivery from Graham McKenzie. That was in Sydney and the accident occurred chiefly because the pitch was over-grassed and had not been prepared enough. A reassuring thought . . .

We won the toss and put them in. It was likely to be a low-scoring match and in that case it is always better to know just how many you have to make; the side batting first often feels anxious and frustrated because runs aren't easy to put together. And then there was rain about.

Willis and Edmonds bowled well into the black stuff and Tasmania, predictably, struggled really hard for runs. It rained – a vote of thanks to the weather station – and quite hard at times, but we stayed on through most of it. Tasmania's innings was reduced to forty-eight overs and they made 131–6, most of their batsmen giving themselves up in frustration because of their inability to score freely. It was a damp dank day and the small crowd hardly filled a corner of the ground.

The heavy showers greased up the pitch and helped the ball seam and bounce when we batted. I appealed against the rain but the umpires insisted on staying put and I got out early when I tried to square cut a delivery which bounced and skidded through. Old Flat Jack took the catch at the second attempt at slip.

Everybody struggled. Some deliveries squatted, others bounced and the rain swept over the ground in swirling mists of great white clouds, very heavy at times. At one stage it rained hard for forty minutes on end but the umpires would not come off – and the match was slipping and sliding towards complete farce. Fielders and bowlers struggled to keep their feet and even batsmen had to tread warily because once the mudflats became wet they clogged the studs in your batting boots. It was like skating.

Not surprisingly, batsmen were very apprehensive and we pushed, poked and prodded our way to victory by three wickets. Hardly the most exhilarating day's cricket but blame the weather and the state of the ground for that. With so much rain about and the constant possibility that the umpires might relent and take the players off, there was the familiar equation about runs and overs to be considered if the match was curtailed. Derek Randall carried a list on a piece of paper, a sort of sliding scale to show how many runs we needed if the weather took hold at certain stages, and he kept pulling it out and peering at it while he was batting. What a performance!

John Hampshire was, of course, a member of the Tasmania side and there was the usual Press interest in our relationship. I asked Kenny Barrington to bowl at me in the nets and Hampshire picked up the ball. 'I'll bowl at you', he said. 'It will give the Press something to talk about.' Nothing more was said.

17 Australia revival

The first one-day international in Melbourne never had a chance of surviving as a spectacle from the moment it was decided to play it on a pitch which had been used for a Shield match only forty-eight hours previously.

After being used for three days – a fourth day was rained off – the pitch was watered and rolled and given one day's rest before the international was played. It had turned during the Shield match; it was hardly likely to be any better for being rolled and watered.

So it proved. It was slow and uneven with an unpredictable bounce. At the pavilion end there were patches of black mud, not even solid mud at that, and when the ball hit a black patch it stopped and jumped. The square was in a dreadful mess, huge areas of black soil, a terrible place to field; Yallop stooped to field a shot from me and the ball leaped off a divot and hit him on the ear: not by any means the perfect pitch for one-day cricket.

Somebody had draped a banner along the southern stand saying 'This is fair dinkum cricket Mr Packer' – and how disappointed they must have been! Australia were bowled out for 101 and we won by seven wickets – and that's not the sort of cricket the fans expect from a limited-overs international. Spectators like to see runs in these matches and no batsman felt free to play shots on that pitch; goodness knows what attendances will be like in the two remaining one-day matches at Melbourne against Australia and the Gillette Cup winners Tasmania, one felt. Cricket lost out badly because of that pitch.

David Bairstow played his first match for England, a necessary blooding in case Taylor suffered an injury late in the tour, and the captain told him before the match started: 'If you

think they're out, let's hear you appeal. Don't be shy, Bluey...'
I made a mental note to send a telegram to the lads back home.
Bairstow shy? They wouldn't stop laughing for a week.

Australia won the toss and batted, which was something of
a relief because we knew runs would be very hard to come by.
I reckoned that a total of 160 would take a bit of beating; anything appreciably higher than that and we would have a real
battle on our hands.

They never looked like getting anywhere near that total. We
bowled tightly and fielded well and it was almost impossible
for batsmen to get the ball away. So they fretted, became worried by their lack of progress and got out to a rash of awful
shots. I could sympathise with their predicament.

Willis bowled really quickly and Hendrick, just the sort of
bowler for this sort of match and conditions, took 4–25 to win
the Man of the Match award and deservedly so. But I was still
disturbed by the bowling of Botham; he was strictly military
medium and a bit loose, flattered by his haul of two wickets.
He rarely fails, because he is a lucky player and nobody would
take that away from him, but he can bowl a great deal better
than he did today.

There were two outstanding dismissals in the Australian
innings, unlucky or brilliant depending on your point of view.
Wood hit Edmonds off the meat of the bat through square
leg and Gower – who had been put there a few minutes previously by the captain – took off to his left to take a magnificent catch shoulder-high: a great combination of instant
reflexes and safe hands. Then Yallop was run out by Randall,
a brilliant piece of fielding considering he was sliding about in
the mudflats when he picked up and threw down the wicket
underarm as Yallop galloped for a quick single. A stop would
have been remarkable, a run-out was simply superb.

England never looked like losing. We lost Brearley early on
and Randall and Gooch got out to poorish shots after playing
quite well. But I played the anchorman's role and Gower
fashioned some good shots when we were close to their total;
we were never in serious difficulty.

*

There was an unpleasant surprise awaiting us when we turned up at the ground to play the rearranged one-day international against Australia. Thieves had got into the dressing room during the night and taken a lot of equipment players had left in the belief that it would be safe and under security.

Poor David Bairstow. He had already lost a fair bit of kit when a large holdall went missing somewhere between Melbourne and Adelaide a fortnight previously, and now one of his bats had disappeared. We estimated about £400 worth of gear had gone, including pads belonging to Old, a sweater of Brearley's, a pair of Randall's gloves, trousers and gloves belonging to Miller and a helmet of Radley's. I had my best bat stolen, which was more than just an inconvenience; it had been specially made and flown out from England and I did not have another as good. Strangely enough, I left four bats in the dressing room, three of them a bit past it autographed by both teams as a souvenir. But the thieves had ignored them and taken only the best one; they obviously knew what they were after and it wasn't just mementoes of the tour! The police came and took details but admitted there was little chance of getting the stuff back: my bat was distinctive because it had a Slazenger motif not used in Australia, but even that wasn't likely to help.

The pitch again looked poor, better than yesterday's with a more solid look to it, but still definitely below par. It was damp – after all, we had played in the rain through much of the previous day – and because the weather was still cool there was little chance for it to dry out. 'The side batting first on that is at an unfair disadvantage,' said Willis – and we would have had no hesitation in putting Aussie in. That is why we opted for five seamers and left Edmonds out. But Australia won the toss and put us in, even though they were without Hogg, who was resting in readiness for the last Test.

We were two down in next to no time. Brearley tried to hook a delivery from Dymock which bounced and hurried into him and was caught behind down the leg-side, then Randall padded off without offering a stroke and was lbw to Dymock.

The ball was already knocking the top off and it was a toss-up whether the next delivery would bounce or squat, dribble through to the wicketkeeper or jump alarmingly. Gooch and I took a couple on the gloves in front of our faces. 'Get yourself a helmet or you'll get hurt,' he said. We battled on towards lunch with singles here and there and a lot of determination. Gooch went after braving it out for an hour, caught low down by Hurst at mid-off, and I was out to the last ball of Laughlin's first over before lunch to a delivery which shot along the ground and hit me just above the boot as I played forward. England 89–4.

The pitch dried out progressively and batting became much easier though there was still a fair amount of frantic stuff, slogs and nicks littered among the good shots. Yallop produced some strange field placings with men half way or three-quarters of the way to the boundary, stranded in no-man's land, and that helped Gower and Botham to pick up runs more easily than they might. They put on 50 in 49 deliveries and after Botham was out Gower went on to make a beautifully mature 101 not out. He needed three for his century off the last ball of the innings, waited while Australia put all their men on the boundary and then coolly found a gap between cover and extra cover for four: every inch the big occasion player enjoying himself.

We finished with 212–6 and that was much better than we expected; a total of 160 to 180 would have been pretty good going in the circumstances so we felt confident we could win it, especially since our bowlers were more experienced in limited-overs competition. The best-laid plans . . .

I don't know whether being left out of the Test squad left a really deep scar, but Darling chanced his arm from the start and was soon out, cutting for a change, for seven. Hughes and Wood gradually got the scoreboard ticking over, putting on 48 in thirteen overs before Wood was bowled by a slower delivery from Old, and already Hughes looked in decent form. He played several good shots with the full face of the bat and might have pushed the score along faster except that Yallop became bogged down and could not give him enough of the strike. Australia desperately needed some momentum at that stage and Yallop could not provide it; the crowd began to get after him and it looked as though Aussie had little hope of gearing themselves up for a win.

Hughes made 50 in twenty-one overs and was looking to get on with it when he hoisted Lever straight to me at long-on. But rather than let the innings fade, Toohey determined to play his shots from the outset. He slogged when he had to and played sensibly when he could – and Yallop gradually began to play a few shots of his own.

They ran for practically everything and it soon became noticeable that they were taking two to some of our best fielders. They were galloping, we were under pressure in the field and there was an air of mild bewilderment as the runs flowed steadily. But they were still behind the required scoring rate: 145–4 in the thirty-second over when Yallop was out and I sensed a feeling that we had only to play them along to win in the end. Gary Cosier was in no mood to be patronised.

Cosier is a big, square man with immense strength and a good eye. He faced only fourteen deliveries in twenty-four minutes, but his innings made all the difference as far as Australia's confidence was concerned. And he turned in twenty-eight runs which swung the match decisively at that stage.

Not to put too fine a point on it, he knocked seven kinds of sawdust out of the bowling. He hit Botham over mid-off for four, hoisted Lever for an enormous six over long-on – surely one of the biggest hits ever seen on the massive MCG – then made room to bang a four over cover which was only a foot or so from being another huge six. It was scientific slogging and great improvisation, and as Toohey chipped twos and threes with a batsman's eye two overs produced twenty-nine runs.

Suddenly Aussie were racing away with the match. The crowd got behind them – they hadn't had too much to cheer during this series – and once the batsmen sensed they were on top they hit harder and harder, more and more confidently. Laughlin hurled Lever for a straight four and six off successive deliveries, Toohey straight-drove Willis imperiously for four and Australia piled on 50 in 5.3 overs on their way to victory by four wickets. And we had started the innings so confidently.

So what went wrong? I felt we did not pressure them long enough. We had them tied down in the first 25 overs or so when we set our fields to save one, but then we spread the field and bowled a strange sort of line, on or outside the leg stump to leg-side field placings.

That gave Hughes and Toohey far too many free hits for comfort, so that although they were scoring at only five or six an over and that wasn't enough, they were growing in confidence all the time. Once a batsman feels confident and aggressive it is difficult to nail him down again; their innings was allowed to gather momentum like a great stone rolling downhill. And once Cosier had finished, the stone was going too fast to be halted.

Brearley and the bowlers had several conferences and it seemed Botham had this notion that it was impossible to bowl straight without being slogged on an easy pitch. So he bowled to a 6–3 leg-side field and Hendrick had five on the leg and four on the off, which was extraordinary when you consider his great strength is a nagging length just outside off stump.

My feeling has always been that bowlers in those circumstances should bowl straight. If they miss, you hit, and even if the ball is over-pitched it can only be hit in the V between long-off and long-on. If the ball is straight and full length it is very difficult to get it away without taking risks and improvising a lot: the batsman who knows he can have a swing without being bowled if he misses has a fair weight taken off his mind.

As a first principle I think line and length is worth persevering with. If batsmen do get away and are going too well, then the point of attack may have to be changed, but I felt we began to experiment and compromise before Aussie forced us to.

Lever is usually a very good bowler at the death because he pitches it well up, and I think he struggled so badly because he hasn't had a lot of match bowling. Cosier and Laughlin took him to pieces because he didn't bowl a full enough length; that is how they were able to get so much height on their big shots.

Australia's victory meant a third one-day match was arranged at MCG three days later. And that just about coincided with the news that two senior umpires had reported the ground as being unfit for first-class cricket!

If Australia needed a lift before the final Test they certainly had one in the third one-day international at Melbourne. They took the Benson and Hedges series beating England by six wickets – and we never really looked like winning the match.

The toss was vitally important, perhaps too important, again. Yallop has a habit of winning it, or perhaps one should say that Brearley has developed a habit of losing it since he does the calling while Yallop does the spinning. Sure enough, Yallop won the toss again and put us in, not surprisingly since the pitch was firm and a little damp.

We were soon in obvious trouble. The ball seamed, swung in the overcast, English sort of atmosphere and bounced unpredictably early on – hardly the best sort of surface for limited-overs cricket. Dymock got one to bounce at me and I was caught at gully off my glove, Randall was caught at slip off his first ball and then Gooch got one which bounced from Hurst and was taken at slip. In no time at all we were 17–3 and when Gower played an airy sort of stroke to Wood at point England were 22–4 and really struggling.

Brearley battled along, determined to keep the innings from collapsing completely and Botham hit three fours – one off the edge and two off the middle – in a fifth wicket partnership which put on 20. But Botham finally went to a poor shot, dragging the ball on to his stumps as he drove Cosier without using his feet, and the scene was set for the most bizarre dismissal of the match.

Brearley drove Cosier through midwicket and he and Bairstow set off for a run ... and another ... and another. In fact they had run five when Carlson's return from the far distance bounced over the wicketkeeper's head! Brearley called for a sixth and although he had galloped a couple of yards past the wicket at the far end Bairstow turned and set off gamely with all of twenty-five yards to cover. He and the throw from Hughes arrived at the non-striker's end at much the same time and although Bairstow felt he had made it because he thought Cosier broke the wicket before the ball arrived, the umpire thought otherwise. An odd way of getting out to say the least – and a very unnecessary one with the match slipping from us as fast as it was.

Brearley practically carried the innings off his own bat, 46 out of a total of 94, without a great deal of help from anyone. Edmonds batted very well for 15 when every run was precious and made his point forcibly when the Aussie bowling became blatantly negative.

Laughlin set a 6–3 offside field and bowled wide of the off stump, a favourite little ploy of his. So Edmonds plucked out the leg stump and knocked it in three feet wide of the off stump in protest – a cool piece of heavy sarcasm which was lost on nobody. The umpire had to replace the stump and three deliveries later Edmonds on the front foot was given out lbw to Laughlin.

All we needed to have a chance of winning was a miracle – and we hadn't been blessed with too many of those. Unless we got wickets early there was little hope of defending 94 runs, and Wood and Darling got off to a flying start with twenty off the first two overs. They played and missed a bit and skinned a knuckle or two but it was a bold, positive start: 50 inside 12 overs despite the loss of Darling and then Hughes, caught at mid-off, driving too early at Willis.

Botham bowled round the wicket at Wood to try and keep the runs down and we switched our bowlers looking for variety and a way through. But Yallop steadied the Aussies, survived a few awkward moments and made 25 before he was bowled by a full toss as he aimed a very fine drive on the off-side. Toohey played nicely again and Cosier hit the winning run, much to the delight of the locals.

We lost three out of four matches against Australia at Melbourne, so it was hardly our favourite ground. And in each case the toss was chiefly responsible for the result; whoever won the toss won the match, which is an annoying reflection on the state of the pitches.

The results in the one-day matches must have lifted Australia's confidence for the last Test, and Yallop was quoted as saying he thought they might do quite well in the World Cup competition, having beaten a very experienced one-day side. They do have their weaknesses but I still don't think they are as weak a side as many people have been making out.

18 The last post

Perhaps it was all rather academic – the chances of Mike Brearley actually winning the toss seemed to get longer by the minute – but we had a long discussion about the best decision, just in case. It was a difficult one. The day before the match the pitch was dry and cracked; this morning it was damp, having been watered to bind it together. But would it do enough to bowl a side out on the first day? It turned during the previous Test at Sydney and there were spots at one end which dusted up if you rubbed them with a finger; after five days and a rest day it should turn quite a bit. Ponder, ponder.

Australia won the toss and batted. Brearley lost his eighth toss out of nine calls in six Tests and three one-day matches, having called tails at Brisbane and heads the rest of the time. Perhaps he should call something else!

Wood set off at the gallop with boundaries off Willis, but Hilditch was rather less sure of himself, understandably in his first Test. Anxiety and nervousness probably launched him into a run despite the fact that Gooch had made a diving stop at gully and despite Wood's twice-repeated refusal. Gooch threw as he sprawled on the ground, Hilditch finally got the message and tried to get back and there was a brief panic before Emburey ran him out. Gooch's throw missed the stumps, bounced just in front of Emburey who was backing up and hit him on the shin. Fortunately it dropped in front of him and he just had time to pick it up and break the wicket before Hilditch arrived.

Hendrick and Willis bowled accurately on a good line and length outside the off stump and neither Wood nor Hughes could get the ball away easily. They fretted and eventually Wood was drawn forward defensively by Hendrick and edged a catch which Botham took brilliantly, very low and wide of his right hand.

Yallop got the bouncer treatment from Willis, but we reckoned Hendrick was the bowler most likely to get him out, as he did twice in the Adelaide Test. So Hendo plugged away at him for eighty minutes against a stiff breeze, although it had been our intention originally to use the quicker bowlers in short bursts. Yallop saw it through and gradually began to score more confidently, especially against Botham who ran in downwind but did not bowl particularly well; he was chopped, edged, cut and driven for boundaries.

Hughes played and missed almost as often as he middled the ball and escaped luckily when a delivery from Willis beat him and nicked the off stump without dislodging a bail. But they kept the score ticking over until Willis came back on for the last over before lunch and Hughes edged a widish delivery to Botham at second slip. Australia 61–3 and we reckoned we had done a good morning's work.

The captain wanted Hendrick and Willis to attack again after lunch; one more wicket and we were through to Carlson and into the tail. Hendrick bowled very well against Toohey – still the favourite with customers on the Hill – but Yallop didn't seem to have much trouble with Botham.

He cut and straight drove and when Botham went round the wicket, Yallop whacked him over midwicket with a characteristic shot, a sort of pick-up with a full follow-through and a straight bat. He made his 50 out of 97–3 in a little over two hours; very valuable runs.

As soon as Toohey got to Botham's end he was caught behind pushing forward, and the new arrival, Carlson, didn't seem to have much idea what was going on. He played at least four deliveries as though he hadn't seen them and when Botham dug in a quicker one, Carlson simply fended it off the splice to third slip. Half the Australian side out for 109.

Yardley likes to have a go, but after one wild cut at Botham which sailed over first slip for four he pulled his horns in a bit and tried to play responsibly. Emburey winkled him out. Yardley never seemed happy against him and eventually got his left foot too far across to the arm ball which pitched leg and middle and hit leg stump.

The spinners always seem to give Wright more trouble than the seamers. He was out bat-pad in the last Test propping forward defensively and he appeared nervously aware of the ring of close fielders and tried to get down the wicket to drive. Emburey bowled him a slower, flighted delivery and Wright had begun to advance before he realised he could not get to the pitch of the ball. He jabbed at it, squeezed it between bat and pad and as it rolled behind him he was stumped expertly by Taylor.

Poor Yallop was running out of partners fast. He looked in fine form himself, positive and confident, rarely wasting the chance to hit a loose delivery. He was particularly severe on Emburey, perhaps because Emburey has a higher loop than Miller and the wind drifted the ball on to Yallop's legs, giving him time to pick his spot and hit high and handsome over the top. Yallop thumped several fours over mid-on and wide long-on, square cut for threes and swept when Emburey pitched leg stump.

Hogg tried hard to stay there for his captain's sake. He was cajoled and encouraged all the time but he never looked very permanent playing the spinners defensively, and soon after tea he fell to Miller. It was a slower ball, floating out and drawing Hogg towards extra cover, then turning and flicking off bat and pad to Emburey at short square leg. A classic little spinner's wicket.

Yallop was approaching a century and probably deserved one but we made him work hard for it all the same. A risky single to mid-off suggested he was getting a bit frustrated, then he pushed to cover and galloped for his 100th run. Gooch fumbled it or Higgs would probably have been run-out.

Once he cleared that hurdle, Yallop banged Emburey over wide mid-on for four and tried to lift Miller over mid-off. But he never got to the pitch of the ball and skied it to mid-off, where Brearley seemed to have it covered all the way – until the wind took it away at the last moment and Mike could only get his fingers on it.

Yallop was going far too well for comfort and Brearley suggested I bowl a few, try and keep it tight until the new ball nine overs away. I said it would be better to bring back one of the seamers, probably Botham, give Yallop singles and try to bowl Higgs out. But I bowled one over and almost had Higgs stumped, in fact Taylor thought he had got him as he played and missed and then overbalanced.

Botham finally came on for Miller and Yallop, trying to hoist him on the leg-side again, banged the ball straight to Gower at square leg. The end of a super innings; 121 priceless runs made in very difficult circumstances.

A pause for drinks and then Botham promptly yorked Hurst with a delivery which just dislodged a bail. Botham's analysis just about summed him up. He was expensive – 57 runs off 9.7 overs which is six an over – yet he took four wickets, more than anyone else in the innings! He really is an extraordinary performer.

Australia 198 all out; Brearley and I made 24 before the close. We both felt and probably looked in good shape; I got off the mark with a cover-driven four off Hurst and the captain drove, swept and cut confidently. He had one escape off Yardley, playing forward defensive he was dropped at slip by Hughes who went too far to his left for it and let the ball hit his wrist.

Second day
One delivery from Hogg which kept low and another which jumped and took the top off suggested it wasn't going to be easy. The patches at one end are small but they are worn and will deteriorate as the match goes on: good news for the spinners. Hogg tried really hard and Hurst varied his attack with characteristic determination, but we made a steady enough start until I edged one towards second slip.

I turned away, convinced that the ball had bounced fractionally before it reached the fielder, but Hilditch and the rest of the slips – not to mention all the Aussies within half a mile – claimed it as a catch. I indicated to the umpire that I thought it had bounced, but he decided it was out so I set off straight away.

Carlson had already replaced Hogg, who only likes to bowl in four-over spells, but Hogg was recalled to have a go at Randall, the new batsman. He dropped one short and Randall pulled it through midwicket for four, then he bowled one which kept a bit low and hit the inside edge before thumping the pad. Randall clearly thought he had hit the ball when he was given lbw – and no wonder since the nick was heard all over the ground. Strangely enough, Brearley said at lunch that he did not hear the nick at the other end. So perhaps the umpire was faced with a tricky one.

It was slow going at first – Brearley took fifty minutes to score his first run of the day and acknowledged the jeers with a touch of his cap – but he and Gooch played themselves in steadily against Yardley and Carlson. There was one bizarre incident in an expensive over from Yardley when Gooch late cut for four, hit him very straight for another four and then cut him off the back foot for three behind square. Wright, the Australian wicketkeeper, appealed to both umpires for a hit-wicket decision against Gooch, claiming that he had dislodged the off bail as he played his shot. In fact, though he did not realise it, Wright himself disturbed the leg bail as he took the return. Gooch didn't think he had touched the bails and it seemed some time before anyone noticed that the wicket had been broken.

Brearley off-drove Carlson for four, his best shot of the morning, and had something of an escape when he helped a slow bouncer from Carlson on its way and the ball fell just short of Hurst at fine leg. England lunched at 98–2.

Derek Randall took his wife on to the Hill after lunch. It's the sort of daft thing he would do, a bit like stepping into a lions' den except that Derek would probably make the lions laugh. He was recognised, of course, somebody thrust a drink into his hands and a fair little party started. And naturally everybody fell about laughing when a couple of girls decided the Randalls looked a bit hot and threw a bucket of water over them ...

It was a mystery why Higgs had not bowled before lunch, especially since Yardley took a fair bit of punishment; I thought that a couple of overs with men round the bat would have been worth exploring. He and Hogg opened the attack after lunch and scoring was never easy against them, though Gooch pulled Hogg for four off his hip and Brearley ran his twos and threes. Brearley did not look happy against Higgs.

Some deliveries spun into him and he jabbed at the ball, not quite timing his strokes. Eventually he drove at Higgs, did not get to the pitch of the ball and lofted a catch to Toohey running forward at cover. England 115–3.

Runs came quickly now, as Gooch played some fiercely confident shots and Gower played as only he can, chancing his arm but playing some wonderfully inventive and effortless strokes. Gooch sailed past his previous best total on tour, 43, and the partnership put on 67 in 49 minutes against Hurst, Higgs, Hogg and Yardley before Gooch tried to drive a widish delivery from Yardley and Wright made a lightning stumping as the ball turned past the bat. Gooch played well, hitting the ball very hard as he does when he's in form – one shot off Yardley was a massive straight six which hit the terracing and bounced half way back to the pitch!

Botham played back to his first ball from Higgs and edged it between wicketkeeper and first slip for two – it was strange that Higgs should bowl to only one slip and with nobody round the bat against the new batsman, especially since Botham hasn't played him well in the past. Botham attempted to cut a short ball and top-edged it high over slip for three; he played off bat and pad more than once but there was nobody close enough to take advantage. The field placings mystified me and I don't know what Higgs himself must have thought about them; certainly it couldn't do much for his confidence. Even when it was obvious that Botham was struggling a bit against the spinners, Yardley bowled at him with only one slip. I found it hard to understand.

The ball was obviously turning now and Higgs bowled a very good over to Gower round the wicket into the rough, tempting him. One delivery turned a lot and tucked him up; the next spun in the crease and Gower had to kick it away. We passed Australia's total and were 216–4, a lead of 18, at tea.

The light had not been good for the last half hour as a storm approached from the direction of Botany Bay. It broke as tea was taken, fierce and quite spectacular at its height, and in no time the outfield was a lake of puddles. The wind was cold and gusty and at one stage it was impossible to see the Hill from the pavilion as the rain lashed down. It did not last long but the ground was awash and no play was possible for the rest of the day. Well, almost no play. The Ockers from the Hill played their own fifty-a-side match on the outfield, splashing and body surfing through the puddles – probably as wet inside as they were soaked outside.

Third day

The morning was full of possibilties for Australia now that the ball was turning a bit, and after twenty-five minutes they took the wicket they wanted when Botham tried to hit over the top and holed out to Carlson at mid-off. They had made the breakthrough, there was obviously something in it for the spinners and Australia had the new ball available. And still their reluctance to attack, the lack of men round the bat, was extraordinary.

Yardley gave Miller quite a bit of trouble and Higgs, bowling round the wicket, pitched into the rough and kept Gower quiet. Gower cut a short one for four but then Higgs pitched a googly in the rough, it bounced but didn't turn much, and Gower gloved it to the wicketkeeper. England 247–6.

Yallop finally put pressure on Taylor – short square leg, slip and gully for Higgs – but I thought his tactics were still a bit strange. Miller played bat and pad several times to Yardley and Higgs yet there was no man square or just in front of square on the off-side.

And when Taylor faced Yardley there was a fielder stationed six or seven yards from the bat at silly mid-off. Unless Taylor is a contortionist there is no way the ball would be pushed or bat-padded there!

Australia took the new ball after eighty overs with England 265–6, and four overs later Hurst trapped Miller lbw for 18. It nipped back quite a way and hit the front pad; Miller thought it might have done too much.

Emburey was out quickly, chasing a widish one and offering a shoulder-high catch which Hilditch did well to reach and hold at second slip, but Willis was determined to stay around while Taylor pushed and worked for runs. Hogg sometimes bowled off his short run and pitched in the occasional off-spinner, Hurst varied his deliveries as shrewdly as ever, but the batsmen were maddeningly defiant. An hour produced 34 runs, mostly from Taylor, who was playing well again – not exciting cricket perhaps but a very important period for both teams. Every run could be vital.

Willis had played the survival game magnificently while Taylor ferreted on, but he was out after batting valiantly for seventy minutes. He tried to sweep Higgs but the ball pitched in the bowlers' rough well outside the leg stump and turned viciously to bowl him middle and off stump. Hendrick went soon afterwards and England finished their innings on 308 with a lead of 110.

On that pitch such a lead was priceless. Batsmen might be criticised for going slowly but only by those who did not recognise the demands of the situation or the sheer difficulty of scoring quickly when the ball turns and spinners bowl accurately. Higgs forced so many bat-pad shots that he might have had a lot more wickets, though Yardley was not as tight as he has been. He is difficult to drive on the ground because of the way he loops his deliveries, but players seem to have worked him out and hit him over the top more now. He also gives more room to cut. It was slow going but it was absorbing cricket – even if one customer with a trumpet insisted on playing the Last Post and Hogg confessed during a break for drinks that he was 'bored to death'.

We opened with Willis and Hendrick but didn't expect them to bowl for long. Clearly, the spinners were the danger men now. Hendrick gave us a bonus with the wicket of Hilditch – but the circumstances were very unfortunate.

Hilditch played defensively at a wide one and got a fine edge. The ball went down but Taylor dived forward, reached it at full stretch and the slips around him went up for a catch. Poor Bob wasn't too enthusiastic; I don't suppose he could be certain whether he had caught it or not but from where I was standing it did not look like a catch. Hilditch was stunned when he was given out, trailing off disconsolately. Later in the dressing room he was in tears. To make matters worse, the TV replay suggested it wasn't a catch at all.

Hughes and Wood scored fairly freely off the seamers, but once the spinners came on it was a different match. Botham dived but could not quite reach a bat-pad by Hughes off Emburey, but two deliveries later Gooch stuck out his left hand at short leg and Australia were 28–2. The two left-handers, Wood and Yallop, dug in. They couldn't score but they seemed determined to stay there, ringed by fielders, trying to kill the spin before it killed them. Interestingly, Miller and Emburey were bowling at opposite ends from the first innings – but the same ends from which they had bowled Australia out in Sydney in the fourth Test.

Wood had an escape on 21, looping a catch off his boot to Brearley at gully but surviving a confident appeal. He had made another eight when he tried to drive Miller very firmly through mid-on and got a leading edge. The ball sailed high over the cover area where Willis turned, ran and judged a difficult catch to perfection as it came over his shoulder. Australia 48–3 and the start of a decisive collapse.

Toohey missed his first delivery and edged a bat-pad catch to Gooch at short leg next ball. Then Carlson pushed forward firmly at his second delivery and plonked a catch into the hands of Botham at short square leg. Australia 48–5.

The trumpeter on the Hill was playing the 'Last Post' again and in the adjoining showground Rod Stewart's backing group were tuning up for a concert later that night. It was either very tuneful or a horrible racket depending on your taste in music; either way it did little for the batsmen's concentration and Yallop asked the umpires if they could have it stopped. Word was sent to Cold Chisel to cool it and the trumpeter was asked to tone it down a bit. He wandered off with his (empty) esky, let rip into 'When the Saints Go Marching In' as he walked round the ground and played a few mournful tunes before the peal died away.

Yallop played well again – defensively, of course, not getting the ball away – and Yardley, as ever, was defiantly aggressive. Brearley widened the field for him and I suggested we should put mid-off back, too; he likes to whack the ball and if we had mid-off back it could be four or out. Yardley used his feet well, getting down the pitch and driving for singles with the field spread.

I suggested Emburey went round the wicket to Yardley and

in the last over of the day he did so. Yardley padded off without playing a shot and the ball in my opinion would have hit middle stump. He was lucky to survive the appeal.

Australia finished the day 70–5, still forty behind and they didn't have much hope on that pitch. Nobody can play a shot with confidence; batsmen try to survive but they know they will get a good one sooner or later. Test pitches should turn but this was the third day and the ball was already turning a hell of a lot. It simply was not a Test match pitch, though I appreciate that with all the State, Test and W.S. cricket the groundsman had more pitches to prepare than usual.

Fourth day

It was gloomy and overcast with a spot of rain in the wind – please don't let it rain now! – when Australia set out on their impossible mission. Yardley began sketchily and would have been run out had Brearley gathered the ball cleanly; Yallop soon went when one turned and he got a fine edge pushing half forward. Taylor was so quick to gather the ball and whip off the bails that both umpires gave Yallop out, caught behind and stumped!

Yardley tried to get down the pitch to the spinners as he had the previous day, but he didn't find that too easy against Miller, who saw him coming once or twice and who bowls flattter in any case. He was more successful against Emburey, who bowls with a bigger loop and does not like to go round the wicket; Yardley off-drove him or steered him behind point.

After fifty minutes Hendrick replaced Emburey, chiefly for variation's sake, bowling very tight with an off cutter thrown in from time to time. I was beginning to think that if we didn't get another wicket soon we might change the spinners' ends when Wright swept Miller and I caught him just behind square leg. He had done well trying to survive under pressure, but it was desperately difficult to get the ball away.

Australia 114–7; Hogg got off the mark with a Chinese cut for three and then concentrated simply on staying there while Yardley put runs together. Hendrick and Emburey switched a couple of times and even Yardley couldn't slog the slower ball or the cutter. He took a chance when he pulled a good-length delivery for three to reach his 50, but most of the time he concentrated on keeping the strike away from Hogg. On that pitch it was impossible.

Miller eventually confronted Hogg, who pushed through the ball as he has so often done against the spinners and was bowled middle and leg. Australia needed a miracle; they had only Higgs and Hurst.

Higgs became the orthodox offspinners' victim on a turning pitch, caught at short square leg off bat and pad, and although they prolonged their innings past lunch it did not last long after that. Hurst gave a straightforward return catch to Miller and Australia were 143 all out. England needed 34 to win.

There was a delay before our innings started because Yallop wanted to open his bowling attack with an old ball and for some strange reason the umpires were determined to let him. Weser came in, told Brearley what was in the wind and said, 'You've no objections, have you?' I thought Mike was going to blow up. He was really angry, rightly so, and he insisted the laws said a new ball must be taken if either captain wanted it at the start of an innings. We weren't likely to agree to an old ball with the pitch turning square. They went back to see Yallop and they returned to our dressing room some minutes later.

The umpires said they couldn't trace the law.* Our manager Doug Insole spelled it out to them. But they still reckoned Yallop was entitled to an old ball if he wanted one. The manager made it clear that if the Australians were allowed to use an old ball a formal complaint would be made – although, of course, a complaint would not help our batsmen, who would be put at an unfair disadvantage.

Yardley opened to me with four men round the bat. The top had gone off the pitch and the ball turned and bounced alarmingly. I let it hit me on the body twice and the fielders round the bat appealed like madmen. Here we go again . . .

We both used our pads to Yardley a fair bit, played and

* *Laws of Cricket* (B) 5: '. . . Subject to agreement to the contrary, either captain may demand a new ball at the start of each innings . . .'

missed, steered a few and edged a few, got in a few firm drives. Hard going. Brearley late cut Higgs for four, tried twice more but missed because he was trying to hit the ball too hard; I on-drove Yardley for three. Higgs bowled several deliveries wide of the leg stump because the pitch was terribly scuffed in that area and the ball did all sorts of things. It was safe enough to pad up there and I did so several times – and nearly got deafened by the appeals for lbw! Finally I tried to hit off the back foot, the ball turned and bounced and through trying to hit too hard I spooned a catch to cover off the top face of the bat. Soon afterwards Brearley hit Yardley over midwicket for the winning runs. England's series 5–1.

This business about the old ball really was infuriating. I wonder if Yallop was simply being awkward – and he ought not to have got away with it, even though they were both standing in their first Test match.

There have been turning pitches in Australia before but nobody could remember a previous example of an innings opening with an old ball.

19   Conclusion

Doug Insole told us at the end of the tour that this was an England team which could make a very great impact on world cricket in the next few years; you can never tell.

Great sides have come and gone in Test cricket; sides which looked as though they would last forever have disintegrated surprisingly quickly and apparently modest teams have achieved minor miracles in the game. I am a great believer in the theory that a season – one Test series – is a long time in a player's career; it is dangerous and unwise to try to plan too far ahead, to project what that player or this side will be like in a few months. Cricket is a game which often defies prediction.

But I don't go along with the idea that the side has peaked and will become progressively less effective from now on. It may do; only time will tell. But I do feel there is a lot left in the squad which did so well in Australia – and I include the old men in that assessment!

Bob Willis and I did not do as well as we hoped or many people expected, and I can already hear the critics saying that one or both of us is over the hill in terms of England performance. It is not necessarily a carping criticism, often an objective view from observers who know that change is important to the well-being and development of well-rounded Test sides.

But the most objective critics sometimes underestimate the value of seasoned experience in a Test side. I don't think Yallop would underestimate it – in fact I suspect he would give a great deal for a bit of help and guidance along the way – but whilst England is winning there is bound to be a move to push youth and young flair for its own sake. Fair enough, but let nobody underestimate the degree to which the younger players appreciate and need the guidance of older heads, even if those older heads are not breaking records or setting matches alight themselves. Test cricket is, to a degree, about knowledge and experience and the English selectors have always recognised that.

That is why men like Doug Insole and Kenny Barrington have such a beneficial influence on tour sides abroad; that is why experienced batsmen and bowlers can contribute so much to the effectiveness of a side without pulling up forests of trees themselves. The younger players, full of talent and potential, need older shoulders to lean on; sometimes in terms of runs and wickets and sometimes in terms of advice and coaching. It's not an easy game.

This was undoubtedly the best England fielding side with which I have ever played. I don't think I let anybody down in the outfield and there was no weak link in the side – most unusual when you consider that several of the great sides have had to hide a donkey or two among the greyhounds. Two players set the tone and the standard, and a superb standard at that – Gower and Randall, magnificent in key fielding positions, an example and a challenge to the rest of the team.

We took good catches and sometimes brilliant ones, and at last we have quick bowlers – not normally famous for their agility in the field – who can produce a consistently high standard in the slips or close positions. Old, Botham and Hendrick are very fine close fielders and Willis is certainly no slouch at slip when he is given the opportunity. Edmonds is a brilliant close fielder, Miller and Emburey are perfectly proficient and Lever has a superb arm. The list could go on; I defy anyone to name an England player in Australia who had to be nursed or hidden in the field. In fact I suspect the Aussies were a bit taken aback. They are used to fielding young sides who give the geriatric Poms a lesson or two round the field; suddenly they were faced with a side who could field as well and more often better than they could. It was quite a blow to Aussie pride.

Our bowling strength in numbers and consistency was an important factor; we were out to win matches and the contribution of so many bowlers became a vital factor in our ability to put pressure on and to keep it on. England had five bowlers who took between 16 and 23 wickets in Test matches; Australia relied heavily on Hogg, Hurst and Higgs and crossed their fingers that others might weigh in with a performance or two.

Australia lost three Tests, Perth, Sydney and Adelaide in that order, which they might have won and went down heavily in the series. And hell hath no fury, as they say, like an Aussie beaten. Their Press was vitriolic in condemning the team as incompetent or worse; it became a popular bleat that England were playing the second eleven while the stronger Australian team played in the World Series Cricket circus. Well, that might be an easy excuse in a country which enjoys its victories and needs to explain its defeats away – but the facts simply do not support that view.

It must be remembered that in 1977 England had already thumped an Australian side composed largely of current World Series players and that several Packer men – Ian Chappell and Ian Redpath for instance – came out of retirement only when Packer's series was launched; they had already been lost to established Australian cricket.

I suspect the Australians underestimated the ability of the England side – and rather than admitting that they rubbished their own players mercilessly. It was a short-sighted and unfair policy, especially at a time when a largely untried Australian side needed all the encouragement it could get, and it gave the Australian public a distorted view of the players who represented them.

There were other reasons for Australia's defeat and if the series was disappointing as a spectacle there were reasons for that too.

Who could deny that the pitches were below standard for Test cricket? Batting was something of a lottery, especially for the high-order batsmen in both sides; we were facing the new ball and the fast bowlers when they were fresh; and if the Australians failed pretty consistently, so did experienced England players.

I am certain that Test cricket is basically about batting. At some stage in the game the bat has to dominate; bowlers will always take wickets, especially Test-class bowlers in a five-day situation, and so batsmen need some sort of dispensation from the kind of pitches on which they are asked to play. The pitches on this tour accentuated the element of luck and fluke to the point where no batsman could be sure of his ground. The great Bradman himself once remarked that nobody expected Joe Davis to play snooker on a bumpy table ... yet in this series Test batsmen were expected to overcome inadequate pitches.

The great uncertainty of cricket is all very well but it should hinge on the ability of one side to force mistakes or another side's susceptibilty to make them – not on the state of the pitch in match after match. Groundsmen in Australia were obsessed with the need to make pitches last five days and so produced strips which had a lot of grass on them and which tended to be damp on the first day, and that meant that the toss became excessively important; the side batting first was always likely to be at a disadvantage.

When we commented about the amount of grass on the nets at Adelaide – and they were among the best – the groundsman said; 'I can take the grass off but they won't last very long', and the same philosophy was applied to Test pitches.

Even the outfields were lush and damp, good to look at perhaps, but quite unnecessary for Test cricket. Dry, fast outfields in Australia can add thirty runs to a day's play and that improves the spectacle without falsifying the action; considerations like that can go a long way towards making Test matches more attractive for spectators.

Then there was the umpiring. Perhaps I shall be accused of complaining unnecessarily but let me make it clear that the standard of umpiring was the same for both sides; both England and Australia suffered equally. Overall, the umpiring on this tour did not in my opinion measure up to the high standards required for Test and other first-class cricket which I have enjoyed the last sixteen years.

The reluctance of players to go when given out, dissent which attracts a lot of publicity – wrong though it most certainly is – arose in my opinion from uncertainty about the basis of decisions.

Players on both sides were criticised – and, in my view, quite rightly – for the excessive amount of appealing which developed in Test matches. Some of it, made with absolute conviction by players who must have known that a decision simply was not on, was quite unjustified. Such appeals arose, I think, from uncertain umpiring and in the expectation that some were bound to succeed. Some of us on both sides were unhappy about the trend.

I believe that English umpires, most of them former professionals themselves, would not have put up with it. They would have told the players to cool it and perhaps proved their point by dismissing a close decision with a knowing stare; there are ways and means to put an end to irresponsible appeals without losing respect – indeed in such a way as to increase authority.

These standards were not achieved. The umpires could have taken a leaf out of Tom Brooks' book – an authoritarian who is not above talking to players and winning their confidence – but they assumed an air of infallibility which their decisions did not always bear out.

In writing as I have I do appreciate that umpiring is a difficult job, especially on pitches where the ball is always 'doing a bit', and I am not underestimating the pressures. But I do feel that umpiring had an effect on some players during the tour and since we were accused of failing to entertain it is only fair to mention this as being a factor which I believe led to uncertain batsmanship by both teams.

I have made brief references to bouncers which caused no serious problem on this tour. I refer to bouncers again simply to state my view that the laws are clear and only need to be applied rigorously by the umpires. This will avoid unpleasantness and dissension on the field and create a better atmosphere which will transmit itself to the spectators.

I think I should refer to the cross chat which occurs, on the field, from time to time around the batsmen. At times this is extremely unpleasant and no holds are barred in an attempt to break concentration; I have referred, earlier in this book, to one example of this which did not disturb me unduly because I have acquired the habit of concentrating and of being able largely to ignore the kind of thing that goes on.

At times I suppose some of the cross chat can be humorous but it is sometimes peppered with bad language and occasionally it has been known to be of a cruel nature – obviously in those cases where a really determined effort has been made to upset the batsman.

Such action, by either fielding side, is not good enough; it is a sneaky type of gamesmanship, directed at the batsman, often unheard by either of the umpires, who are well away from the batsman's end of the wicket, and only usually used when the fielding side is facing a difficult situation and desperate to break through.

Such gamesmanship, which has never, within my knowledge, been adopted by the best captains and the greatest players, is simply not good enough and should be eradicated. Once again its eradication rests in the hands of the umpires, who would undoubtedly have the full backing of authority if they were to take the steps which should be taken.

Equally I hold the view that the modern habit of back slapping and hugging, whenever a wicket is taken, which has crept into the game over the last few years, is a bad thing; it has no part in my book and, I fell sure, is generally considered, as currently practised, to be somewhat effeminate – though the practice I believe is equally distasteful to most spectators. I know that some people feel that such congratulations help team spirit and, certainly, for a splendid piece of work, in the field, by the batsman or by the bowler, the generous applause of fellow players – even opponents – is to be encouraged; but not love and kisses which is what some spectators consider the current practice to approach!

A lot is expected of captains in Test cricket and I decided early in the tour that we had a head start in pitting Mike Brearley's ability and experience against that of Graham Yallop. I know I was not proved wrong.

I watched Brearley pretty closely – naturally I had a keen professional interest in doing so; everybody's captaincy fascinates me – and I consider he did a magnificent job on and off the field. His batting might not have been all that startling but both of us went through a thin spell. His captaincy was first-rate.

It is easy to claim that Brearley was leading a good side against a poor one but that is too facile an argument; his record is excellent and nobody can do better than achieve the job they set out to do. Let's face it, you cannot get a much better result in Australia than 5–1. The facts speak for themselves.

And let me make one thing clear, just in case it is necessary. I have no complaints at all about Mike's attitude towards me. I know some people were looking for a so-called personality clash and have been since Mike returned as captain. Well, I'm not sorry to disappoint them. Before the Perth Test match I considered that Mike was not making full use of my experience and I told him and Doug Insole that I felt I could have a useful contribution to make, and after that – once he knew how much of a contribution I really wanted to make – Mike was great. I liked the way he asked my advice, quietly and sensibly, not with some great expansive gesture to let the world know how fair he was being to Geoff Boycott. We just got on with the job as professionals and I respected him for that.

The experienced competence of Mike Brearley threw into contrast the inexperience of Graham Yallop; for whilst Brearley spoke cautiously in public simultaneously giving his team quiet confidence, Yallop, publicly optimistic on numerous occasions, then found himself unable to obtain the requisite response, dedication and effort from his players.

I must refer to the fact that the nature of Australian crowds at cricket has changed dramatically since 1970–71. The majority of Australians like their sport; they like to win but they can take it when they lose. But there is a ten per cent element in the crowds these days who are, alas, the worst I have ever met in cricket.

The Hill at Sydney used to be amusing, sharp and cutting but not unfriendly; now it is simply foul-mouthed and crude. Ockerism is a way of life for many young Australians – it's a hard term to define but it means enjoying a reputation for being brash, hard, basic and unsophisticated – and those who make the most noise usually make it in four-letter words. I reckon they let their country down – and that is a shame because the (silent) majority still know how to enjoy and appreciate real Test cricket.

I came in for some special treatment from the Ockers on most grounds. I can take it – after all my years in the game I'm not unaccustomed to abuse – but I confess I found it a bit wearing on top of difficult pitches and nagging problems with decisions. And then, of course, there was the Yorkshire situation ...

I tried not to let it prey on my mind; after all, I had a job of work to do in Australia, but it was a deeply depressing situation. I will never know just how much it affected my performance and I am not going to use it as any sort of excuse, but the loss of the Yorkshire captaincy and the way it was effected certainly hurt, and the controversy raging at home didn't help me concentrate on playing Test cricket. Perhaps if Yorkshire were just a job the whole situation wouldn't have affected me quite as much, but Yorkshire is an emotional thing for me. That's why I decided to accept the club's offer of a two-year contract.

I am the sort of person who tends to bottle things up and I must say how grateful I am to Doug Insole. He showed a great deal of understanding and sympathy, went out of his way to talk to me about things and offer whatever help and advice he could. I really appreciated that.

And it was warming to receive so much support and encouragement from the Australian public as well as thousands of well-wishers from home. Not the Ocker Australians I have already mentioned, but the majority who are fair-minded and dislike seeing a man kicked when he is down. The harder the Australian Press thumped me, the more letters I received from Australians, most of whom I shall never meet, saying they understood my situation. Perhaps young people who have never faced real emotional difficulties find it hard to appreciate other people's problems; the Ockers will learn and the majority of Australians sympathised. That was a great help.

186

It was a difficult tour for me, emotionally, and psychologically. Whatever the blemishes – I'm bound to say I feel proud of the part I played. I tried to contribute in every match, I like to think I played an important part in winning two Test matches and above all, I proved that I am not a quitter. There were plenty of critics waiting to suggest I was, to show that I couldn't really take it. They have done so before and perhaps nothing will change their view, but those who waited for me to fold and give it away misjudged and misread the man.

Put to the Test ... perhaps I didn't entirely fail.

1st MATCH v. SOUTH AUSTRALIA COUNTRY XI

Played at Renmark, November 1st. Match drawn.
England XI 199–4d (G.A. Gooch 47, C.T. Radley 64, J.M. Brearley 29). South Australia Country XI 137–6 (A.J. Sampson 37, I.J. Fillery 35).

2nd MATCH v. SOUTH AUSTRALIA

Played at Adelaide, November 3rd, 4th, 5th, 6th. South Australia won by 32 runs.

SOUTH AUSTRALIA

J. E. Nash	lbw b Miller	124	st Taylor b Miller	33
W. M. Darling	c Miller b Willis	17	c Edmonds b Old	1
I. R. McLean	c Taylor b Edmonds	30	c sub (Randall) b Miller	52
B. L. Causby	c Brearley b Miller	20	c & b Edmonds	0
J. N. Langley	st Taylor b Edmonds	1	st Taylor b Edmonds	4
†R. K. Blewett	c Taylor b Willis	22	b Edmonds	12
P. R. Sleep	c Taylor b Lever	45	c Taylor b Edmonds	3
‡T. J. Robertson	c Taylor b Willis	2	b Edmonds	24
R. M. Hogg	b Lever	11	run out	16
G. R. Attenborough	lbw b Miller	19	run out	3
A. T. Sincock	not out	14	not out	1
Extras	(B2 LB2 NB2)	6		—
Total		311		149

ENGLAND XI

G. Boycott	lbw b Hogg	9	lbw b Hogg	62
G. A. Gooch	c Robertson b Hogg	23	b Sleep	4

England XI v. South Australia

England XI — Batting

Batsman	First innings	Runs	Second innings	Runs
D. I. Gower	lbw b Attenborough	50	c Blewett b Sincock	73
†J. M. Brearley	b Sincock	25	run out	27
‡G. Miller	c Langley b Hogg	5	lbw b Sincock	0
R. W. Taylor	c Blewett b Sleep	4	c Langley b Attenborough	6
P. H. Edmonds	not out	28	c Robertson b Attenborough	38
J. K. Lever	c & b Sleep	0	b Hogg	1
C. M. Old	c Darling b Sleep	40	c McLean b Sleep	4
R. G. D. Willis	absent hurt	—	not out	0
Extras	(LB5 NB8)	12	(B4 LB1 NB7)	13
Total		**196**		**232**

Bowling

ENGLAND XI	O	M	R	W	O	M	R	W
Willis	11	1	61	3	12	2	40	0
Lever	16	1	67	3	9	1	20	1
Old	18	2	78	0	16	2	37	2
Miller	18.4	5	41	3	21	3	52	5
Edmonds	21	5	53	2				
Gooch	1	0	5	0				

S. AUSTRALIA	O	M	R	W	O	M	R	W
Hogg	12	2	43	4	12.4	1	39	2
Sincock	9	0	42	1	10	0	28	3
Attenborough	15	1	49	3	11	2	49	2
Sleep	17.5	3	72	3	12.5	1	49	2
Blewett	10	4	13	0	5	1	19	0

FALL OF WICKETS

	SA 1st	E 1st	SA 2nd	E 2nd
1st	31	9	11	19
2nd	133	15	55	22
3rd	195	148	64	67
4th	196	148	64	100
5th	200	149	84	108
6th	245	179	90	117
7th	261	215	112	117
8th	272	222	144	124
9th	281	232	146	192
10th	311	—	149	196

3rd MATCH v. VICTORIA COUNTRY XI

Played at Leongatha, November 8th. England XI won by 71 runs. England XI 130–8d (G. Miller 30, G. A. Gooch 29, C. Aitken 4–30). Victoria Country XI 59 (S. McNamara 20, J. E. Emburey 5–10).

4th MATCH v. VICTORIA

Played at Melbourne, November 10th, 11th, 12th, 13th. Match drawn.

VICTORIA

J. M. Wiener	c Edmonds b Lever	48
P. A. Hibbert	c Tolchard b Old	6
D. F. Whatmore	c Edmonds b Lever	27
†G. N. Yallop	b Edmonds	10
P. Melville	c Edmonds b Emburey	16
J. K. Moss	c Emburey b Edmonds	73
T. J. Laughlin	run out	37
‡I. L. Maddocks	c Radley b Edmonds	8
I. W. Callen	c Tolchard b Emburey	8
A. G. Hurst	b Emburey	1
J. D. Higgs	not out	1
Extras	(LB15 NB4)	19
Total		254

J. M. Wiener	not out	16
P. A. Hibbert	not out	14
	(NB3)	3
	(0 wkts.)	33

ENGLAND XI

†J. M. Brearley	not out	116
G. A. Gooch	lbw b Hurst	3
D. W. Randall	b Wiener	63
D. I. Gower	c & b Wiener	13
C. T. Radley	c & b Higgs	22
‡R. W. Tolchard	c Whatmore b Higgs	0
P. H. Edmonds	c Melville b Higgs	5
C. M. Old	c Maddocks b Hurst	4
J. E. Emburey	c Higgs b Laughlin	5

J. K. Lever............... } did not bat
M. Hendrick ....
Extras .... (LB3 W2 NB5) 10

Total .... (8 wkts. dec.) 241

BOWLING

ENGLAND XI	O	M	R	W		O	M	R	W
Old............	17	5	44	1		4	1	3	0
Lever............	18	3	52	2					
Hendrick	11	2	29	0		2	0	3	0
Edmonds	22	6	48	3					
Emburey	26.5	5	56	3		5	0	11	0
Gooch	2	0	6	0					
Randall						2	0	9	0
Radley						1	0	4	0
VICTORIA									
Hurst............	17	4	44	2					
Callen	16	4	44	0					
Higgs	39	8	82	3					
Laughlin............	15.7	5	24	1					
Wiener	13	3	31	2					
Yallop	2	0	6	0					

FALL OF WICKETS

	V 1st	E 1st	V 2nd
1st	11	7	—
2nd	84	121	—
3rd	93	145	—
4th	113	195	—
5th	129	199	—
6th	213	207	—
7th	239	225	—
8th	244	241	—
9th	249	—	—
10th	254	—	—

5th MATCH v. AUSTRALIAN CAPITAL TERRITORY

Played at Canberra, November 15th. England XI won by 179 runs.
England XI 225-2 (40 overs) (G. Boycott 123*, R. W. Tolchard 108). ACT 76 (33.6 overs) (B. Willett 32, R. G. D. Willis 4-10, M. Hendrick 2-7, G. Miller 2-5).

6th MATCH v. NEW SOUTH WALES

Played at Sydney, November 17th, 18th, 19th, 20th. England XI won by 10 wickets.

ENGLAND XI

G. Boycott	not out	14
G. A. Gooch	not out	66
D. W. Randall	c Border b Lawson	110
C. J. Radley	c Rixon b Border	13
D. I. Gower	c Hughes b Clews	26
G. Miller	c Hughes b Border	5
I. T. Botham	b Hourn	56
‡R. W. Taylor	st Rixon b Hourn	9
J. E. Emburey	c Toohey b Clews	0
†R. G. D. Willis	c Hilditch b Lawson	21
M. Hendrick	c Johnston b Lawson	20
Extras	b Border	34
	(B17 LB6 W2 NB9)	

Total	(0 wkts.)	374

NEW SOUTH WALES

J. Dyson	c Boycott b Miller	67
†A. M. Hilditch	c Taylor b Willis	4
P. M. Toohey	c Gower b Hendrick	23
A. R. Border	c Taylor b Miller	11
D. A. H. Johnston	c Hendrick b Miller	16
G. C. Hughes	c Hendrick b Miller	27
M. L. Clews	st Taylor b Emburey	1
‡S. J. Rixon	c Hendrick b Miller	10
G. G. Watson	c Boycott b Emburey	2
	c Gooch b Willis	6
	b Botham	93
	c Gooch b Botham	20
	c Taylor b Botham	12
	c Gooch b Botham	3
	c Emburey	11
	run out	5
	c Botham b Emburey	24
	not out	14

N.S.W. (batting, 1st)			N.S.W. (2nd)	
G. F. Lawson	not out	0	c Miller b Willis	0
D. W. Hourn	c Emburey b Miller	0	b Botham	0
Extras	(LB1 NB3)	4	(B6 LB4 W1 NB4)	15
Total		165		210

(stray figures: 7, 0, 15, 210)

BOWLING

N.S.W.	O	M	R	W
Lawson	17	5	39	3
Watson	18	2	61	0
Clews	13	1	88	2
Hourn	32	4	114	2
Border	12.1	2	38	3

ENGLAND XI	O	M	R	W	O	M	R	W
Willis	8	3	16	1	15	3	39	2
Hendrick	12	2	33	1	4	6	4	0
Botham	9	2	41	0	17.2	6	51	5
Miller	18.4	3	56	6	24	6	56	0
Emburey	10	4	15	2	22	5	44	2
Gooch					1	0	1	0

FALL OF WICKETS

	E 1st	NSW 2nd	NSW 1st	E 2nd
1st	20	5	18	—
2nd	145	47	57	—
3rd	173	65	82	—
4th	250	107	87	—
5th	252	142	119	—
6th	276	146	124	—
7th	305	162	173	—
8th	313	165	192	—
9th	336	165	209	—
10th	374	65	210	—

7th MATCH v. QUEENSLAND COUNTRY XI

Played at Bundaberg, November 22nd. England XI won by 132 runs.
England XI 259–5 (35 overs) (J. M. Brearley 59, R. W. Tolchard 74, D. W. Randall 37, G. A. Gooch 32*), Country XI 127 (31.6 overs) (K. Maher 47, P. H. Carlson 31, J. K. Lever 4–17, G. Miller 2–15, P. H. Edmonds 2–6).

8th MATCH v. QUEENSLAND

Played at Brisbane, November 24th, 25th, 26th, 27th. England XI won by 6 wickets.

QUEENSLAND

M. J. Walters	c Gower b Willis	4
W. R. Broad	c Taylor b Old	0
A. D. Ogilvie	retired hurt.	45
G. J. Cosier	c Taylor b Botham	0
P. H. Carlson	c Miller b Old	37
T. V. Hohns	c Taylor b Willis	43
††J. A. Maclean	c Boycott b Botham	94
G. K. Whyte	c Brearley b Old	0
G. Dymock	c Brearley b Botham	16
L. F. Balcam	not out	21
G. W. Brabon	lbw b Old	1
Extras	(NB16)	27
Total		289

retired hurt. 0
lbw b Willis 41
(7) c Gower b Willis 43
(3) b Willis 32
(4) b Botham 1
(5) c Old b Botham 3
(8) c Gooch b Old 1
(6) b Botham 10
c Taylor b Botham 13
b Botham 10
not out 2
(B4 LB2 NB21) 16

172

ENGLAND XI

G. Boycott	c Cosier b Brabon	6
G. A. Gooch	c Brabon b Dymock	34
D. W. Randall	c Maclean b Balcam	66
‡R. W. Taylor	c Maclean b Dymock	2
†J. M. Brearley	not out	75
D. I. Gower	b Balcam	6
G. Miller	c Maclean b Dymock	18
I. T. Botham	c Maclean b Dymock	6

c Maclean b Balcam 60
c Ogilvie b Carlson 22
b Whyte 47

not out 38
c Cosier b Hohns 1
not out 22

ENGLAND XI (contd.)				
C. M. Old	lbw b Balcam			2
P. H. Edmonds	c Maclean b Cosier			14
R. G. D. Willis	b Brabon			6
Extras	(B7 LB2 NB9)			18
Extras	(B1 LB3 W1 NB14)			19
Total				208
Total	(4 wkts)			254

BOWLING

ENGLAND XI	O	M	R	W		O	M	R	W
Willis	11	1	40	2		11	1	46	3
Old	14.7	4	33	4		14.2	3	63	1
Botham	12	1	66	3		20	0	70	5
Gooch	3	0	11	0		1	0	8	0
Edmonds	5	2	6	0		8	1	35	0
Miller						11	1	40	0

QUEENSLAND	O	M	R	W		O	M	R	W
Balcam	13	1	56	3		12	2	25	1
Brabon	10.1	1	45	2		5	0	31	1
Carlson	14	1	48	0		9.3	1	29	0
Dymock	19	3	46	4		17	5	38	1
Hohns	2	0	3	0		8	5	13	0
Cosier	4	0	19	1		5	2	10	0
Whyte	7	3	18	0		15	3	44	1

FALL OF WICKETS

	Q 1st	E 1st	Q 2nd	E 2nd
1st	4	14	0	42
2nd	90	75	0	117
3rd	97	90	83	165
4th	100	129	83	168
5th	129	148	121	—
6th	135	188	169	—
7th	158	201	214	—
8th	159	208	268	—
9th	172	241	289	—
10th	—	254	—	—

FIRST TEST MATCH

Played at Brisbane, December 1st, 2nd, 3rd, 5th, 6th. England XI won by 7 wickets.

AUSTRALIA

Batsman		Dismissal	Score		Dismissal	Score
G. M. Wood		c Taylor b Old	7	lbw b Old	19
G. J. Cosier		run out	1	b Willis	0
P. M. Toohey		b Willis	1	lbw b Botham	1
†G. N. Yallop		c Gooch b Willis	7	c & b Willis	102
K. J. Hughes		c Taylor b Botham	4	c Edmonds b Willis	129
T. J. Laughlin		c sub (Lever) b Willis	2	lbw b Old	5
‡J. A. Maclean		not out	33	lbw b Miller	15
B. Yardley		c Taylor b Willis	17	c Brearley b Miller	16
R. M. Hogg		c Taylor b Botham	36	b Botham	16
A. G. Hurst		c Taylor b Botham	0	b Botham	0
J. D. Higgs		b Old	1	not out	0
Extras		(LB1 NB6)	7	(B9 LB5 NB22)	36
Total			116		339

ENGLAND

Batsman		Dismissal	Score		Dismissal	Score
G. Boycott		c Hughes b Hogg	13	run out	16
G. A. Gooch		c Laughlin b Hogg	2	c Yardley b Hogg	2
D. W. Randall		c Laughlin b Hurst	75	not out	74
R. W. Taylor		lbw b Hurst	20		
‡J. M. Brearley		c Maclean b Hogg	6	c Maclean b Yardley	13
†D. I. Gower		c Maclean b Hurst	44	not out	48
I. T. Botham		c Maclean b Hogg			

G. Miller	lbw b Hogg	27
P. H. Edmonds	c Maclean b Hogg	1
C. M. Old	not out	29
R. G. D. Willis	c Maclean b Hurst	8
Extras	(B7 LB4 NB7)	
Total		286

17
170
(B12 LB3 NB2)
(3 wkts)

FALL OF WICKETS

	A 1st	E 1st	A 2nd	E 2nd
1st	2	2	0	16
2nd	5	38	2	37
3rd	14	111	49	74
4th	22	120	219	—
5th	24	120	228	—
6th	26	215	261	—
7th	53	219	310	—
8th	113	226	339	—
9th	113	266	339	—
10th	116	286	339	—

BOWLING

ENGLAND	O	M	R	W	O	M	R	W
Willis	14	2	44	4	27.6	3	69	3
Old	9.7	1	24	2	17	1	60	3
Botham	12	1	40	3	26	5	95	3
Gooch	1	0	1	0				
Edmonds	1	1	0	0	12	1	27	0
Miller					34	12	52	2

AUSTRALIA	O	M	R	W	O	M	R	W
Hurst	27.4	6	93	4	10	4	17	0
Hogg	28	8	74	6	12.5	2	35	1
Laughlin	22	6	54	0	3	0	6	0
Yardley	7	1	34	0	13	1	41	1
Cosier	5	1	10	0	3	1	11	1
Higgs	6	2	9	0	12	1	43	0

10th MATCH v. WESTERN AUSTRALIA

Played at Perth, December 9th, 10th, 11th. England XI won by 140 runs.

ENGLAND XI

Batsman	First Innings		Second Innings	
G. Boycott	lbw b Clark	4	c Marsh b Yardley	13
G. A. Gooch	c Wright b Alderman	3	c Wright b Porter	15
C. J. Radley	b Alderman	2	c Marsh b Yardley	18
†J. M. Brearley	c Wright b Porter	11	b Yardley	18
D. I. Gower	c Wright b Alderman	0	c Marsh b Porter	4
‡R. W. Tolchard	not out	61	b Yardley	3
I. T. Botham	c Charlesworth b Porter	21	c Marsh b Yardley	4
P. H. Edmonds	lbw b Porter	22	c Wright b Alderman	27
J. E. Emburey	c Wright b Clark	6	not out	7
J. K. Lever	c Wright b Mann	8	b Alderman	1
M. Hendrick	c Charlesworth b Mann		b Clark	8
Extras	(B1 LB2 W1 NB4)		(B7 NB1)	8
Total		144		126

WESTERN AUSTRALIA

Batsman	First Innings		Second Innings	
G. M. Wood	b Lever	2	lbw b Botham	15
R. I. Charlesworth	c Tolchard b Botham	3	lbw b Lever	6
K. J. Hughes	b Botham	8	lbw b Botham	1
G. R. Marsh	c Tolchard b Botham	0	c Tolchard b Hendrick	9
†R. J. Inverarity	c Tolchard b Hendrick	9	lbw b Botham	2
A. L. Mann	c Botham b Hendrick	3	c Tolchard b Botham	0
G. D. Porter	c Brearley b Hendrick	8	c Tolchard b Hendrick	2
B. Yardley	c Tolchard b Hendrick		not out	8
				28

	First Innings		Second Innings	
‡K. J. Wright	c Brearley b Botham		b Hendrick	0
W. M. Clark	not out		run out	1
T. M. Alderman	c Botham b Hendrick		run out	2
Extras	(LB3 W1 NB4)	8	(LB2)	2
Total		52		78

BOWLING

W. AUSTRALIA	O	M	R	W	O	M	R	W
Alderman	12	4	18	3	9	2	26	2
Clark	16	4	50	3	12	2	22	1
Porter	17	4	37	3	16	9	16	2
Yardley	2	0	7	0	13	1	54	5
Mann	8.3	2	24	2				
ENGLAND XI								
Lever	8	3	10	1	7	3	16	1
Botham	9	3	16	4	13.5	4	37	4
Hendrick	5.4	2	11	5	7	2	23	3
Gooch	2	0	7	0				

FALL OF WICKETS

	E 1st	WA 1st	E 2nd	WA 2nd
1st	7	4	23	22
2nd	7	6	41	22
3rd	13	10	58	28
4th	17	16	63	32
5th	25	28	69	32
6th	31	39	73	35
7th	69	48	98	48
8th	115	49	115	64
9th	121	49	117	69
10th	144	52	126	78

11th MATCH v. WESTERN AUSTRALIA COUNTRY XI

Played at Albany, December 13th. England XI won by 69 runs.
England XI 208-4 (40 overs) (G. A. Gooch 112, G. Boycott 29). Country XI 139 (34.3 overs) (R. Miguel 53, Ditchburn 31, P. H. Edmonds 4-68).

SECOND TEST MATCH

Played at Perth, December 15th, 16th, 17th, 19th, 20th. England XI won by 166 runs.

ENGLAND

G. Boycott	lbw b Hurst	77
G. A. Gooch	c Maclean b Hogg	1
D. W. Randall	c Wood b Hogg	0
†J. M. Brearley	c Maclean b Dymock	17
D. I. Gower	b Hogg	102
I. T. Botham	lbw b Hurst	11
G. Miller	b Hogg	40
‡R. W. Taylor	c Hurst b Yardley	12
J. K. Lever	c Cosier b Hurst	14
R. G. D. Willis	c Yallop b Hogg	2
M. Hendrick	not out	7
Extras	(B6 LB9 W3 NB8)	26
Total		**309**

	lbw b Hogg	23
	lbw b Hogg	43
	c Cosier b Yardley	45
	c Maclean b Hogg	0
	c Maclean b Hogg	12
	c Wood b Yardley	30
	c Toohey b Yardley	25
	c Maclean b Hogg	2
	c Maclean b Hurst	10
	not out	3
	b Dymock	1
	(LB6 NB8)	14
		208

AUSTRALIA

G. M. Wood	lbw b Lever	5
W. M. Darling	run out	25
K. J. Hughes	b Willis	16
†G. N. Yallop	b Willis	3
P. M. Toohey	not out	81
G. J. Cosier	c Gooch b Willis	4
‡J. A. Maclean		

	c Taylor b Lever	64
	c Boycott b Lever	5
	c Gooch b Willis	12
	c Taylor b Hendrick	3
	c Taylor b Hendrick	0
	lbw b Miller	47

Batsman	1st innings		2nd innings	
B. Yardley	c Taylor b Hendrick	7	c Botham b Lever	12
R. M. Hogg	c Taylor b Willis	0	b Miller	18
G. Dymock	b Hendrick	6	not out	11
A. G. Hurst	c Taylor b Willis	5	b Lever	5
Extras	(LB7 W1 NB2)	11	(LB3 W4 NB4)	10
Total		161		190

BOWLING

AUSTRALIA	O	M	R	W	O	M	R	W
Hogg	30.5	9	65	5	17	2	57	5
Dymock	34	4	72	1	16.3	2	53	1
Hurst	26	7	70	3	17	5	43	1
Yardley	23	1	62	1	16	1	41	3
Cosier	4	2	14	0				

ENGLAND	O	M	R	W	O	M	R	W
Lever	7	0	20	1	8.1	2	28	4
Botham	11	2	46	0	11	1	54	0
Willis	18.5	5	44	5	12	1	36	1
Hendrick	14	6	39	2	8	3	11	2
Miller	16	6	31	1	7	4	21	3

FALL OF WICKETS

	E 1st	A 1st	E 2nd	A 2nd
1st	3	8	58	8
2nd	3	34	93	36
3rd	41	38	93	58
4th	199	60	135	58
5th	219	78	151	141
6th	224	79	176	143
7th	253	100	201	143
8th	295	128	201	147
9th	300	185	206	15
10th	309	190	208	161

13th MATCH v. SOUTH AUSTRALIA

Played at Adelaide, December 22nd, 23rd, 24th. Match drawn, with scores level.

SOUTH AUSTRALIA

J. E. Nash	c Tolchard b Old	10	lbw b Emburey	25
W. M. Darling	c Tolchard b Old	19	(7) not out	41
I. R. McLean	c Tolchard b Gooch	7	(2) c & b Emburey	25
B. L. Causby	b Old	87	(3) c Randall b Emburey	7
R. J. Parker	c & b Edmonds	51	(4) c Randall b Emburey	42
†R. K. Blewett	c Old b Emburey	19	c Brearley b Emburey	51
P. R. Sleep	not out	31	(5) c Tolchard b Old	18
‡S. R. Gentle	lbw b Lever	1	not out	21
A. T. Sincock	not out	12		
G. R. Attenborough				
D. Johnston				
Extras	(LB3 NB1)	4	(LB1)	1
		---		---
Total	(7 wkts dec.)	241	(6 wkts dec.)	231

ENGLAND XI

G. Boycott	c Gentle b Sincock	4	(11) not out	7
G. A. Gooch	st Gentle b Causby	20	(5) st Gentle b Blewett	64
C. T. Radley	c Gentle b Attenborough	60	lbw b Attenborough	1
‡R. W. Tolchard	run out	72	lbw b Johnston	6
D. W. Randall	c Gentle b Attenborough	47	(2) c Blewett b Johnston	45
J. M. Brearley	not out	18	(1) c Parker b Johnston	26
†G. Miller	not out	2	(6) not out	68
C. M. Old			(7) b Attenborough	2

	1st innings		2nd innings	
P. H. Edmonds	....	2		
J. E. Emburey	....	0	(8) lbw b Blewett	
J. K. Lever	....	11	(9) b Blewett	
		6	(10) c Darling b Attenborough	
Extras	(B3 LB4 NB4)		(B1 LB2 NB3)	11
Total	(5 wkts dec.)	238	(9 wkts)	234

BOWLING

ENGLAND XI	O	M	R	W		O	M	R	W
Lever	16	2	63	1	....	10	1	33	0
Old	18	2	55	3	....	5	0	21	1
Gooch	6	1	16	1	....	4	0	11	0
Emburey	17	3	48	1	....	26	3	67	5
Edmonds	17	3	55	1	....	28	9	91	0
Miller					....	4	1	6	0
Boycott					....	1	0	1	0
S. AUSTRALIA									
Attenborough	13	5	41	2	....	16	1	92	3
Johnston	8	2	21	0	....	7	0	44	3
Sincock	5	0	27	1	....	5	0	39	0
Causby	6	0	34	1	....				
Sleep	12	1	58	0	....	2	0	22	0
Blewett	8	1	41	0	....	7	0	35	3
Nash	1	0	1	0	....				

FALL OF WICKETS

	SA 1st	E 1st	SA 2nd	E 2nd
1st	25	26	45	65
2nd	36	32	57	68
3rd	38	138	58	74
4th	129	186	96	91
5th	174	231	140	180
6th	220	—	184	187
7th	221	—	—	196
8th	—	—	—	202
9th	—	—	—	223
10th	—	—	—	—

14th MATCH v. AUSTRALIA (ONE-DAY)

Scheduled for December 26th at Melbourne but abandoned without a ball having been bowled.

THIRD TEST MATCH

Played at Melbourne, December 29th, 30th, January 1st, 2nd, 3rd. Australia XI won by 103 runs.

AUSTRALIA

G. M. Wood	c Embury b Miller	100
W. M. Darling	run out	33
K. J. Hughes	c Taylor b Botham	0
†G. N. Yallop	c Hendrick b Botham	41
P. M. Toohey	c Randall b Miller	32
A. R. Border	c Brearley b Hendrick	29
‡J. A. Maclean	b Botham	0
R. M. Hogg	c Randall b Miller	0
G. Dymock	b Hendrick	0
A. G. Hurst	b Hendrick	1
J. D. Higgs	not out	0
Extras	(LB8 NB6)	14
Total		258

b Botham		34
c Randall b Miller		21
c Gower b Botham		48
c Taylor b Miller		16
c Botham b Emburey		20
run out		0
c Hendrick b Emburey		10
b Botham		1
c Brearley b Hendrick		6
not out		0
st Taylor b Emburey		1
(B4 LB6 NB1)		11
		167

ENGLAND

G. Boycott	b Hogg	1
†J. M. Brearley	lbw b Hogg	1
D. W. Randall	lbw b Hurst	13
G. A. Gooch	c Border b Dymock	25
D. I. Gower	lbw b Dymock	29
I. T. Botham	c Darling b Higgs	22

lbw b Hurst		38
c Maclean b Dymock		0
lbw b Hogg		2
lbw b Hogg		40
lbw b Dymock		49
c Maclean b Higgs		10

‡R. W. Taylor	b Hogg	5	c Maclean b Hogg	1
J. E. Emburey	b Hogg	7	not out	0
R. G. D. Willis	c Darling b Dymock	3	c Yallop b Hogg	19
M. Hendrick	not out	0	b Hogg	6
Extras	(B6 LB4 NB9)	24	(B6 LB7 W1 NB6)	19
Total		179		143

BOWLING

ENGLAND	O	M	R	W	O	M	R	W
Willis	13	2	47	0	7	0	21	0
Botham	20.1	5	68	3	15	4	41	3
Hendrick	23	3	50	3	14	4	25	1
Emburey	14	1	44	0	21.2	12	30	3
Miller	19	6	35	3	14	5	39	2
AUSTRALIA								
Hogg	17	7	30	5	17	5	36	5
Hurst	12	2	24	1	11	1	39	1
Dymock	15.6	4	38	3	18	4	37	2
Higgs	19	9	32	1	16	2	29	2
Border					5	0	14	0

FALL OF WICKETS

	A	E	A	E
	1st	1st	2nd	2nd
1st	65	2	55	1
2nd	65	3	81	6
3rd	126	40	101	71
4th	189	52	136	127
5th	247	81	136	163
6th	250	100	152	163
7th	250	101	157	167
8th	251	101	167	171
9th	252	120	167	179
10th	258	143	167	179

FOURTH TEST MATCH

Played at Sydney, January 6th, 7th, 8th, 10th, 11th. England XI won by 93 runs.

ENGLAND

G. Boycott	c Border b Hurst	8	lbw b Hogg	0
†J. M. Brearley	b Hogg	17	b Border	53
D. W. Randall	c Wood b Hurst	0	lbw b Hogg	150
G. A. Gooch	c Toohey b Higgs	18	c Wood b Higgs	22
D. I. Gower	c Maclean b Hurst	7	c Maclean b Hogg	34
I. T. Botham	c Yallop b Hogg	59	c Wood b Higgs	6
G. Miller	c Maclean b Hurst	4	lbw b Hogg	17
‡R. W. Taylor	c Border b Higgs	10	not out	21
J. E. Emburey	not out	0	c Darling b Higgs	14
R. G. D. Willis	c Wood b Higgs	7	c Toohey b Higgs	0
M. Hendrick	b Hurst	10	c Toohey b Higgs	7
Extras	(B1 LB1 W2 NB8)	12	(B5 LB3 NB14)	22
Total		152		346

AUSTRALIA

G. M. Wood	b Willis	0	run out	27
W. M. Darling	c Botham b Miller	91	c Gooch b Hendrick	13
K. J. Hughes	c Emburey b Willis	48	c Emburey b Miller	15
†G. N. Yallop	c Botham b Hendrick	44	c & b Hendrick	1
P. M. Toohey	c Gooch b Botham	1	b Miller	5
A. R. Border	not out	60	not out	45
‡J. A. Maclean	lbw b Emburey	12	c Botham b Miller	0
R. M. Hogg	run out	6	c Botham b Emburey	0
G. Dymock	b Botham	5	b Emburey	0
J. D. Higgs	c Botham b Hendrick	11	lbw b Emburey	3

A. G. Hurst	run out	0		b Emburey		0
Extras	(B2 LB3 NB11)	16		(LB1 NB1)		2
Total		294				111

FALL OF WICKETS

	E 1st	A 1st	E 2nd	A 2nd
1st	18	1	0	38
2nd	18	126	111	44
3rd	35	178	169	45
4th	51	179	237	59
5th	66	210	267	74
6th	70	235	292	76
7th	94	245	307	85
8th	98	276	334	85
9th	141	290	334	105
10th	152	294	346	111

BOWLING

AUSTRALIA	O	M	R	W	O	M	R	W
Hogg	11	3	36	2	28	10	67	4
Dymock	13	1	34	0	17	4	35	0
Hurst	10.6	2	28	5	19	3	43	0
Higgs	18	4	42	3	59.6	15	148	5
Border					23	11	31	1
ENGLAND								
Willis	9	2	33	2	2	0	8	0
Botham	28	3	87	2	10	3	17	2
Hendrick	24	4	50	2	20	7	38	3
Miller	13	2	37	1				
Emburey	29	10	57	1	17.2	7	46	4
Gooch	5	1	14	0				

17th MATCH v. AUSTRALIA (ONE-DAY)

Played at Sydney, January 13th, and abandoned owing to rain.
Australia 17–1 (W. M. Darling 7*, G. M. Wood c Tolchard b Old 6, K. J. Hughes 0*, extras 4, J. K. Lever 0–8, C. M. Old 1–5; M. Hendrick 0–0). England did not bat.

18th MATCH v. NORTHERN NEW SOUTH WALES

Played at Newcastle, January 14th, 15th, 16th. England XI won by 9 wickets.
Northern NSW 223–9d (J. Gardner 59, C. Beatty 62, P. H. Edmonds 3–66) and 166 (R. Neal 44, C. Evans 64, C. M. Old 4–30, P. H. Edmonds 3–49, J. K. Lever 3–24). England XI 163 (J. M. Brearley 66, R. Holland 4–60, M. Hill 3–49) and 230–1 (G. Boycott 117*, Brearley 59, C. T. Radley 55*).

19th MATCH v. TASMANIA (ONE-DAY)

Played at Launceston, January 18th. England XI won by 163 runs.
England XI 240–8 (40 overs) (I. T. Botham 61, D. W. Randall 60, C. T. Radley 44). Tasmania 77 (34.4 overs) (D. A. Boon 15, G. Miller 3–3, P. H. Edmonds 2–16).

20th MATCH v. TASMANIA

Played at Hobart, January 19th, 20th, 21st. Match drawn.

TASMANIA

M. J. Norman	c Taylor b Old	13	b Emburey	43
G. W. Goodman	c Taylor b Old	1	c Taylor b Willis	1
S. J. Howard	c Taylor b Old	13	b Lever	20
I. H. Hampshire	c Taylor b Old	0	not out	46
‡R. D. Woolley	b Old	4	c Radley b Miller	0
†J. Docking	b Emburey	39	not out	2
J. Simmons	c Miller b Old	1		
D. J. Gatenby	b Willis	1		
G. J. Cowmeadow	c Edmonds b Willis	10		
M. B. Scholes	b Miller	10		
G. R. Whitney	not out	0		
Extras	(B5 LB3 NB5)	13	(B2 LB1 NB3)	6
Total		105	(4 wkts)	118

ENGLAND XI

G. Boycott	not out	90
G. A. Gooch	c Goodman b Whitney	14

England XI		
C. T. Radley	c Woolley b Cowmeadow	15
D. I. Gower	b Gatenby	30
‡R. W. Taylor	b Whitney	1
G. Miller	b Gatenby	44
P. H. Edmonds	not out	7
C. M. Old	did not bat	
J. E. Emburey	did not bat	
J. K. Lever	did not bat	
†R. G. D. Willis	did not bat	
Extras	(B4 LB2 NB3)	9
Total	(5 wkts dec.)	210

BOWLING

ENGLAND XI	O	M	R	W	O	M	R	W
Willis	10	1	24	2	4	1	9	1
Old	14	3	42	6	5	2	12	0
Lever	7	3	18	0	8	0	27	1
Emburey	4	3	1	1	6	1	15	1
Miller	3	1	7	1	5	1	18	1
Edmonds					10	3	27	0
Boycott					1	0	4	0

TASMANIA	O	M	R	W
Cowmeadow	16	2	64	1
Whitney	26	3	73	2
Scholes	10	4	40	0
Gatenby	5	1	22	2
Simmons	1	0	2	0

FALL OF WICKETS

	T 1st	E 1st	T 2nd
1st	6	30	3
2nd	20	54	34
3rd	20	99	102
4th	36	102	107
5th	47	187	—
6th	60	—	—
7th	61	—	—
8th	75	—	—
9th	105	—	—
10th	105	—	—

21st MATCH v. AUSTRALIA (ONE-DAY)

— Played at Melbourne, January 24th, England won by 7 wickets.

AUSTRALIA

G. M. Wood	c Gower b Edmonds	28
A. M. Hilditch	c Bairstow b Botham	10
A. R. Border	c Willis b Hendrick	11
†G. N. Yallop	run out	9
K. J. Hughes	lbw b Hendrick	0
P. H. Carlson	c Randall b Willis	11
T. J. Laughlin	c Willis b Hendrick	6
‡J. A. Maclean	c Edmonds b Botham	11
R. M. Hogg	c Botham b Hendrick	4
G. Dymock	c & b Botham	1
A. G. Hurst	not out	0
Extras	(B4 LB2 NB4)	10
Total (33.5 overs)		**101**

ENGLAND

G. Boycott	not out	39
†J. M. Brearley	b Hogg	0
D. W. Randall	c Yallop b Dymock	12
G. A. Gooch	b Carlson	23
D. I. Gower	not out	19

I. T. Botham ....
‡D. L. Bairstow ....
P. H. Edmonds .... } did not bat
J. K. Lever ....
R. G. D. Willis ....
M. Hendrick ....

Extras .... (LB5 NB4) 9

Total (28.2 overs) .... (3 wkts) 102

BOWLING

ENGLAND	O	M	R	W
Willis	8	4	15	0
Lever	5	2	7	0
Hendrick	8	1	25	4
Botham	4.5	2	16	3
Edmonds	7	0	26	1
Gooch	1	0	2	0
AUSTRALIA				
Hogg	6	1	20	1
Dymock	6	1	16	1
Laughlin	5	1	13	0
Carlson	5	0	21	1
Hurst	5.2	1	14	0
Border	1	0	9	0

FALL OF WICKETS

	A 1st	E 1st
1st	27	7
2nd	52	29
3rd	54	69
4th	55	—
5th	76	—
6th	78	—
7th	94	—
8th	99	—
9th	101	—
10th	101	—

FIFTH TEST MATCH

Played at Adelaide, January 27th, 28th, 29th, 31st, February 1st. England XI won by 205 runs.

ENGLAND

Batsman	First Innings		Second Innings	
G. Boycott	c Wright b Hurst	6	c Hughes b Hurst	49
†J. M. Brearley	c Wright b Hogg	2	lbw b Carlson	9
D. W. Randall	c Carlson b Hurst	4	c Yardley b Hurst	15
G. A. Gooch	c Hughes b Hogg	1	b Carlson	18
D. I. Gower	lbw b Hurst	9	lbw b Higgs	21
I. T. Botham	c Wright b Higgs	74	c Yardley b Hurst	7
G. Miller	lbw b Hogg	31	c Wright b Hurst	64
‡R. W. Taylor	run out	4	c Wright b Hogg	97
J. E. Emburey	b Higgs	4	b Hogg	42
R. G. D. Willis	c Darling b Hogg	24	c Wright b Hogg	12
M. Hendrick	not out	0	not out	3
Extras	(B1 LB4 W3 NB2)	10	(B1 LB16 W2 NB4)	23
Total		169		360

AUSTRALIA

Batsman	First Innings		Second Innings	
W. M. Darling	c Willis b Botham	15	(2) b Botham	18
G. M. Wood	c Randall b Emburey	35	(1) run out	9
K. J. Hughes	c Emburey b Hendrick	4	c Gower b Hendrick	46
†G. N. Yallop	b Hendrick	0	b Hendrick	36
A. R. Border	c Taylor b Botham	11	b Willis	1
P. H. Carlson	c Taylor b Botham	0	c Gower b Hendrick	21
B. Yardley	b Botham	28	c Brearley b Willis	0

	1st innings	R	2nd innings	R
‡K. J. Wright	lbw b Emburey	29	c Emburey b Miller	0
R. M. Hogg	b Willis	0	b Miller	2
J. D. Higgs	run out	16	not out	3
A. G. Hurst	not out	17	b Willis	13
Extras	(B1 LB3 NB5)	9	(LB1 NB10)	11
Total		164		160

BOWLING

AUSTRALIA	O	M	R	W	O	M	R	W
Hogg	10.4	1	26	4	27.6	7	59	3
Hurst	14	1	65	3	37	9	97	4
Carlson	9	0	34	0	27	8	41	2
Yardley	4	0	25	0	20	6	60	0
Higgs	3	1	9	2	28	4	75	1
Border					3	2	5	0
ENGLAND								
Willis	11	1	55	1	12	3	41	3
Hendrick	19	1	45	2	14	6	19	3
Botham	11.4	0	42	4	14	4	37	1
Emburey	12	7	13	2	9	5	16	0
Miller					18	3	36	2

FALL OF WICKETS

	E 1st	A 1st	E 2nd	A 2nd
1st	10	5	31	31
2nd	12	10	57	36
3rd	16	22	97	115
4th	18	24	106	120
5th	27	72	130	121
6th	80	94	132	121
7th	113	114	267	124
8th	136	116	336	130
9th	147	133	347	147
10th	169	164	360	160

In Australia's first innings, Darling retired hurt at 0–0 and resumed at 72–5.

23rd MATCH v. TASMANIA

Played at Melbourne, February 3rd. England XI won by 3 wickets.
Tasmania 131–6 (48 6-ball overs) (G. W. Goodman 36, D. J. Smith 25, R. G. D. Willis 2–20, C. M. Old 2–17). England XI 134–7 (43.4 overs) (G. A. Gooch 29, D. W. Randall 22, D. I. Gower 20, R. J. Sheriff 3–16, G. Cowmeadow 2–30).

24th MATCH v. AUSTRALIA (ONE-DAY)

Played at Melbourne, February 4th. Australia XI won by 4 wickets.

ENGLAND

G. Boycott	lbw b Laughlin	33
†J. M. Brearley	c Wright b Dymock	0
D. W. Randall	lbw b Dymock	4
G. A. Gooch	c Hurst b Carlson	19
D. I. Gower	not out	101
I. T. Botham	c Wood b Hurst	31
‡D. L. Bairstow	run out	1
J. K. Lever	not out	16
R. G. D. Willis	} did not bat	
M. Hendrick		
Extras	(B3, LB3, NB1)	7
Total (40 8-ball overs)	(6 wkts)	212

AUSTRALIA

G. M. Wood	b Old	23
W. M. Darling	c Old b Willis	7
K. J. Hughes	c Boycott b Lever	50
†G. N. Yallop	c Gower b Hendrick	31
P. M. Toohey	not out	54
G. J. Cosier	b Lever	28
P. H. Carlson	c Boycott b Lever	0
T. J. Laughlin	not out	15

‡K. J. Wright .... ⎫
G. Dymock .... ⎬ did not bat
A. G. Hurst .... ⎭

Extras .... (LB6 NB1) 7

Total (38.6 overs) .... (6 wkts) 215

BOWLING

AUSTRALIA	O	M	R	W
Hurst	8	1	36	1
Dymock	8	1	31	2
Carlson	8	1	27	1
Coster	8	0	48	0
Laughlin	8	0	63	1
ENGLAND				
Willis	8	1	21	1
Levet	7	1	51	3
Hendrick	8	0	47	1
Old	8	1	31	1
Botham	7.6	0	58	0

FALL OF WICKETS

	E 1st	A 1st
1st	0	7
2nd	7	55
3rd	50	90
4th	89	145
5th	153	185
6th	158	185
7th	—	—
8th	—	—
9th	—	—
10th	—	—

25th MATCH v. GEELONG AND DISTRICTS

Played at Geelong, February 6th. England XI won on a greater run-rate. England XI 165-9 (40 overs) J. M. Brearley 39, C. M. Old 25*, D. I. Gower 21, P. Caulfield 3-28). Geelong & Districts 100-9 (38.6 overs – pitch invaded by crowd) (K. Davis 23, J. E. Emburey 2-13).

26th MATCH v. AUSTRALIA (ONE-DAY)

Played at Melbourne, February 8th. Australia XI won by 6 wickets.

ENGLAND

G. Boycott	c Cosier b Dymock	2
†J. M. Brearley	c Wright b Cosier	46
D. W. Randall	c Hughes b Dymock	0
G. A. Gooch	c Hughes b Hurst	4
D. I. Gower	c Wood b Hurst	3
I. T. Botham	b Cosier	13
‡D. L. Bairstow	run out	3
P. H. Edmonds	lbw b Laughlin	15
J. K. Lever	b Laughlin	1
R. G. D. Willis	c Wright b Cosier	2
M. Hendrick	not out	0
Extras	(LB2 NB3)	5
Total (31.7 overs)		94

AUSTRALIA

G. M. Wood	c Bairstow b Botham	30
W. M. Darling	c Brearley b Willis	14
K. J. Hughes	c Brearley b Willis	0
†G. N. Yallop	b Lever	25
P. M. Toohey	not out	16
G. J. Cosier	not out	8

P. H. Carlson .... ⎫
T. J. Laughlin .... ⎪
‡K. J. Wright .... ⎬ did not bat
G. Dymock .... ⎪
A. G. Hurst .... ⎭

Extras .... (NB2) 2
                                                                            —
Total (21.5 overs) .... (4 wkts) 95

BOWLING

AUSTRALIA	O	M	R	W
Hurst	5	3	7	2
Dymock	6	1	21	2
Carlson	8	2	22	0
Cosier	7	1	22	3
Laughlin	5.7	0	17	2
ENGLAND				
Willis	5	2	16	2
Hendrick	6	0	32	0
Botham	5.5	0	30	1
Lever	5	0	15	1

FALL OF WICKETS

	E 1st	A 1st
1st	10	29
2nd	10	37
3rd	17	54
4th	22	87
5th	42	—
6th	56	—
7th	91	—
8th	91	—
9th	94	—
10th	94	—

SIXTH TEST MATCH

Played at Sydney, February 10th, 11th, 12th, 14th. England XI won by 9 wickets.

AUSTRALIA

Batsman	1st innings		2nd innings	
G. M. Wood	c Botham b Hendrick	15	c Willis b Miller	29
A. M. Hilditch	run out	3	c Taylor b Hendrick	1
K. J. Hughes	c Botham b Willis	16	c Gooch b Emburey	7
†G. N. Yallop	c Gower b Botham	121	c Taylor b Miller	17
P. M. Toohey	c Taylor b Botham	8	c Gooch b Emburey	0
P. H. Carlson	c Gooch b Botham	2	c Botham b Emburey	0
B. Yardley	b Emburey	7	not out	61
‡K. J. Wright	st Taylor b Emburey	3	c Boycott b Miller	5
R. M. Hogg	b Miller	9	b Miller	7
J. D. Higgs	c Emburey b Miller	9	c Botham b Emburey	2
A. G. Hurst	not out	0	c & b Miller	4
Extras	b Botham (LB3 NB2)	5	(B3 LB6 NB1)	10
Total		**198**		**143**

ENGLAND

Batsman	1st innings		2nd innings	
G. Boycott	c Hilditch b Hurst	19	c Hughes b Higgs	13
†J. M. Brearley	c Toohey b Higgs	46	not out	20
D. W. Randall	lbw b Hogg	7	not out	0
G. A. Gooch	st Wright b Higgs	74		
D. I. Gower	c Wright b Higgs	65		
I. T. Botham	c Carlson b Yardley	23		
G. Miller	lbw b Hurst	18		
‡R. W. Taylor	not out	36		

J. E. Emburey .... c Hilditch b Hurst 0
R. G. D. Willis .... b Higgs 10
M. Hendrick .... c & b Yardley 0
Extras .... (B3 LB5 NB2) 10 (NB2) 2

Total .... 308 (1 wkt) 35

BOWLING

ENGLAND	O	M	R	W	O	M	R	W
Willis	11	4	48	1	3	0	15	0
Hendrick	12	2	21	1	7	3	22	1
Botham	9.7	1	57	4				
Emburey	18	3	48	2	24	4	52	4
Miller	9	3	13	1	27.1	6	44	5
Boycott	1	0	6	0				
AUSTRALIA								
Hogg	18	6	42	1				
Hurst	20	4	58	3				
Yardley	25	2	105	2	5.2	0	21	0
Carlson	10	0	24	0				
Higgs	30	8	69	4	5	1	12	1

FALL OF WICKETS

	A 1st	E 1st	A 2nd	E 2nd
1st	18	37	8	31
2nd	19	46	28	—
3rd	67	115	48	—
4th	101	182	48	—
5th	109	233	48	—
6th	116	247	82	—
7th	124	270	114	—
8th	159	280	130	—
9th	198	301	136	—
10th	198	308	143	—

THE NEW SOVIET PSYCHIC DISCOVERIES

HENRY GRIS & WILLIAM DICK

No other country in the world takes parapsychology –
the science of understanding and harnessing the mind –
so seriously as the Soviet Union. And recently reports
have filtered through to the West of astonishing break-
throughs.

Veteran journalists Henry Gris and William Dick made no
less than six separate trips to the USSR to interview
leading scientists, telepathists, psychokinetic mediums,
hypnotists, healers and other researchers – a privilege
never before granted to Western journalists.

In THE NEW SOVIET PSYCHIC DISCOVERIES they
reveal the astounding developments taking place in Russia
today:

* How the famous 'Kirlian Effect' is being used to combat
  cancer, in an exclusive interview with Semyon Kirlian,
  the inventor.

* How Dr Vasili Kasatkin is saving lives after thirty
  years of studying the medical significance of dreams.

* Why Tofik Dadashev, the successor to Stalin's famed
  mind-reader, has taken over as Russia's mind-reader
  par excellence.

* Why Soviet astronomers are determined to be the first
  people on earth to intercept signals from extraterrestrial
  civilizations.

All these facts and many more add up to an awesome
picture of tomorrow's Soviet Union. A nation that, on the
evidence given, regards parapsychology as its latest
weapon of war!

0 7221 4085 1   £1.50

NON-FICTION/COSMOLOGY

THE WAR THAT HITLER WON

ROBERT EDWIN HERZSTEIN

What possessed the German people to embrace Hitler and his politics of mass-murder? Eminent historian Robert Herzstein points to Goebbels' brilliant manipulation of the mass-media as the key to the Führer's success. Goebbels' diabolical propaganda machine exploited every facet of communication – radio, posters, magazines, documentaries, brochures, and spectacular films – in the drive to capture the minds of millions. By the use of patriotic myth and tradition a nation succumbed to mass hypnosis on a scale never before paralleled.

THE WAR THAT HITLER WON is a stunning and penetrating study of the man behind the Third Reich's message to the world. A message that the masses ultimately turned away from, leaving Goebbels and his Nazi elite to a dream that was doomed to fail.

0 349 11679 2   £2.50

HISTORY/ARCHAEOLOGY

And for more exciting fiction read:

FIRE STORM

ROBERT L. DUNCAN

The Japanese 'Red Watch' are the new samurai of international left-wing terrorism: ruthless, blood-hungry young fanatics prepared to kill – and be killed – for the sake of their burning ideals of anarchy and revolution.

When the Red Watch attack one of the ships belonging to the company that troubleshooter Charles Corwin works for, he's under instructions to buy the guerillas off quietly. Or so he thinks. Until he finds that the company has double-crossed him. Suddenly he's accused of a murder he didn't commit, sexually entangled with a beautiful girl bent on revenge, and running for his life from an international big-business conspiracy of horrifying dimensions.

And that's even before the Red Watch strike again. Hitting the huge oil installations at the port of Los Angeles in a Kamikaze mission calculated to set the world on fire. Literally . . .

0 7221 0519 3   £1.10

ADVENTURE/THRILLER

REVENGE OF THE MANITOU

GRAHAM MASTERTON

THE MANITOU RETURNS . . .

Neil stiffened as he saw his son Toby sitting up in bed, staring at him. His small face was white, white as the silvered light from the moon, and his eyes were intense and glittering. He wasn't smiling. He wasn't frowning. His expression was calm and controlled and, because of that, even more frightening. *Eight-year-old boys grin, or cry, or show some feeling*, Neil thought. *Why is he staring at me like that?*

Toby's eyes sparkled with malevolence. His features seemed to shift and change in the moonlight, one transparency laid over another, until he looked like someone else altogether. Someone older, someone infinitely older . . . and someone infinitely evil.

THE MANITOU HAD BEEN VANQUISHED ONCE BEFORE. THIS TIME HE WOULD NOT FAIL.

0 7221 5987 0   £1.10

HORROR

A selection of bestsellers from SPHERE